LAUNCHING RIGHT IN REAL ESTATE

WHAT THEY WON'T TEACH YOU IN PRE-LICENSE SCHOOL

CARLA CROSS, CRB, MA

What Industry Leaders and Top Agents Say About This Book:

I wish I had a book like this to read and discover many of the key points of real estate when I was considering diving into the profession. This book is an easy read and would be very helpful for anyone considering a profession in real estate.

~Patricia Bombard,
Manager, Coach, Arquette & Associates, Realtors, New York

This is a must read for the will-be successful real estate agent. Be sure to also keep it as a reference to review for continued success. All of Carla's points are spot on and truly work.

~Craig Walker,
Keller Williams Realty, Bellevue, Wa.

Launching Right tells you what you may not hear in the interview: The work it takes, the expenses involved, timeframes, challenges, and the business start-up plan you need to succeed.

~Amy Dedoyard,
Managing Broker, Windermere Real Estate, Kirkland, Wa.

Launching Right in Real Estate is a must for anyone thinking about real estate as a career. The author answers the myriad of questions would-be agents ask, and she's straightforward and honest with her answers.

~Mo Anderson,
Former CEO and Vice Chairman of the Board,
Keller Williams Realty

This is really a valuable resource for those considering a real estate career. You did a thorough and honest explanation of the world of a real estate agent.

~**Terrance W. Moore,**
Attorney-at-Law, Hellmuth and Johnson, Edina, MN.

This is a home run! What I would have given to know this upfront. Your decades of experience clearly set you apart.

~**Brian Leavitt,**
Designated Broker, Keller Williams Realty, Bellevue, Wa.

Anyone who has thought about or decided to pursue a career in real estate should consider this book required reading not only as an aid to making that decision but as an ongoing guide to enjoying a more successful and rewarding career in real estate.

~**Andy Mirkovich,**
Retired Commercial Real Estate Broker,
Financial Planner, Sammamish, Wa.

Carla makes the information in Launching Right in Real Estate engaging and creates an easy step by step method for the reader. I wish I would have had this book when I got started!

~ **Rebecca Del Pozo,**
Managing Broker, Trainer,
Keller Williams Realty Puyallup, Wa.

Sales skills are only part of the picture. Success in Real Estate sales also requires systems, structure and discipline. This book gives you all three.

~**Orvel Ray Wilson,**
CSP, CEC, Co-author, Guerrilla Selling

Launching Right in Real Estate does exactly what the title says. Through real-world stories, easy to understand charts, and plain language instruction, veteran real estate pro Carla Cross helps beginning Realtors launch their careers the right way. Her practical guidance will help you avoid common gotchas while accelerating your career. Every career path needs a book like this.

~Don R. Crawley,
Author of The Compassionate Geek

Send requests for information to Noteworthy Publishing, Carla Cross Seminars, Inc., 1070 Idylwood Dr. SW, Issaquah, WA 98027, phone: 425/392-6914, email: carla@carlacross.com,

Web site: https://www.carlacross.com

International Standard Book Number: 978-0-578-76549-5

$24.95

Dedication

To my parents, Bob and Eleanora Garrison. My mother supported my efforts, even when I didn't become a concert pianist, and, instead, became a real estate salesperson! My dad made many sacrifices to see that my sister and I were able to fulfil our dreams, even though no one in his family went to college.

To my many mentors who sometimes saw in me abilities that I didn't know I possessed. To all, thank you!

As I read the dedication, it strikes me, once again, that no one succeeds alone. Think of those who have given you confidence in your abilities, who've coached you through difficult times, who have believed in you when you may not have believed in yourself—and thank them.

Table of Contents

Acknowledgments

This book could not be written without the contributions of the industry insiders who created and/or provided some of the statistical research:

- Steve Francis, Executive Officer of the Association of Real Estate Licensing Law Officials (ARELLO), provided much of the information about licensing requirements.
- The Washington Department of Licensing, Real Estate Division, provided in-depth information concerning licensing statistics.
- The media department of the National Association of REALTORS® contributed research and recommended sources.
- The Economic Research Group of The National Association of REALTORS® conducted research invaluable in guiding real estate professionals to make the right decisions.

Through more than three decades of various real estate activities, I have learned from some of the best in the business—the agents, managers, owners, and trainers with whom I have been privileged to work. A special acknowledgment to the agents of all three of my offices, who provided the most valuable information I pass along in this book. Through their examples of professionalism, they taught me how to spot winners. Finally, a special tribute to the agents quoted here who contributed advice to help you make the best career decision.

There's nothing as valuable as having dedicated experts agree to read your book drafts. Several wonderful real estate professionals, speakers, coaches, and writers agreed to peruse all 240 pages and give me feedback. In fact, these comments were so valuable that several are included in the text. As you can see, they are not all in real estate. I wanted comments from those not in the field to assure the reader would find the explanations and detail here valuable.

- Don Crawley, CSP, DTM, author of 8 books, including *The Compassionate Geek*, is an internationally known speaker and author who brings humanity into the world of technology (https://doncrawley.com). With Don's combination of geek and humanity, he provided insights and questions to illuminate points in the book.

- Craig Walker, technology guru, former salesperson in various fields, in real estate one year; Bellevue, WA. (craig@craigwalker.broker). Craig's input was invaluable. As an agent new to real estate but very experienced in sales, he assured that I covered the right bases and gave the important advice to succeed.

- Patricia Bombard, manager, coach, and salesperson, Arquette & Associates, REALTORS, Camillus, New York (p.bombard14@gmail.com). As a coach and salesperson, Patricia interviews, hires and coaches agents. Patricia brought several important points forward to help readers make the right decisions for them.

- Carolyn Baran, former designated broker, managing broker, Bellevue, WA. (carolynbaran@kw.com). Carolyn reviewed the chapter on licensing requirements. She is an expert on the legal and practical information would-be and new agents need to launch their careers.

- Brian Leavitt, designated Broker, managing broker, Issaquah, WA. A longtime top salesperson, owner, and manager, Brian has interviewed and hired dozens of new agents. He provided comments that helped bring out important points. (brian.leavitt@kw.com)

- Terry Moore, Attorney at Law. Author of the new book, *The Bulldog Guide to Business Divorce*, Terry specializes in handling business disputes. He read the book with an attorney's eye to detail. His comments were insightful, and I've included several in the text for you. (TMoore@hjlawfirm.com).

- Chris Cross, managing broker, Bellevue, WA. A twenty-year sales and management veteran, Chris specializes in residential real estate in Puget Sound. Chris contributed to the chapter on commission splits, giving you advice that will help you translate the sales pitches from the facts on what it costs to be in a particular company.

- Andy Mirkovich, financial planner, former commercial real estate specialist. Not only has Andy achieved exceptional success in those fields, he's also a virtuoso accordionist. Andy has observed many people coming in—and out—of the business, and he read the draft with an eye to fully informing the reader. (amirkovich@cs.com)

- Orvel Ray Wilson, CSP, CEC, executive coach and international speaker. One of the co-authors of the legendary *Guerrilla Marketing* series (57 titles, in 63 languages, 26 million books in print.) For the past year, Orvel Ray has been my coach, suggesting, encouraging, and sometimes prodding me to give it my best! His breadth and depth of knowledge, and his supportive coaching approach, has made all the difference in the quality of this book. (https://guerrillagroup.com/)

A huge thanks to my long-time friend, real estate business associate and editor, Steve Long. Not only is Steve a precise and accurate editor, he knows me so well he can provide guidance for much more than just the technical aspects of writing (even when I really don't want to hear it). Just kidding, Steve. I so appreciate your expertise.

Thanks to all of you for lending your expertise, experience, and intellect.

Before You Read This Book

There's lots of misinformation out there about real estate careers. The big reason: interviewers are looking for people to hire, and the interview serves as a sales pitch. For example, when you interview for position as a real estate salesperson, you'd expect to get a realistic picture of that career. However, much of what you will hear are actually sales presentations designed to get you to join the company.

Another example: you interview with three companies. In each, you're hired after a half-hour interview. That may lead you to think you're special. You conclude that must mean you'll do really well in real estate. The reality: it is hard *not* to get hired.

On a scale of 1-to-10, ten being brutally honest, how honest can I be with you?

If you said "ten", great! I want to give you straight talk so you can make the right decision.

There are unique opportunities in real estate as a career. On the other hand, not everyone is cut out to sell real estate.

- This book will give you the real facts about real estate as a career. Armed with this information, you can decide if this is the career to pursue, you can interview smartly and choose the right company. Also, I've got some tips to launch your career quickly and successfully.

Two Goals of This Book

My first goal is to give you the straight scoop on what it takes to succeed in this business. No fluff—no sales pitches, just the facts, so you can make good decisions. I'll dispel myths about real estate as a career—that misinformation most would-be agents get from those who want to sell them something—a course, a company, or a product.

{See Appendix B for my survey of new agents: their perception and the reality.}

My second goal is to answer common questions of would-be and new agents, such as:

- Should you start your career part time
- Should you find a mentor
- Should you become an assistant before committing to selling real estate
- What to look for in a manager so you get started right
- How to get the information you need during the interview—and separate the sales presentation from the reality
- Do you need a coach, and what to look for
- What are the fatal mistakes new agents make
- Should you join an office with many/few new agents
- Franchise or independent company, which is better for you
- How much will it cost you to start selling real estate
- How much do you need in savings so you get paid before your savings run out
- How much money can you make and when will you start making it
- What tech priorities should you have
- How can you prepare for success before you're licensed so you can hit the ground running your first day in the business
- What do new will-be successful agents do differently to make money fast

Symbols in This Book
to Capture Important Ideas

 I've listed "Big Ideas," concepts important to your success.

 When you see the To Do symbol, you'll know it's an action or series of actions to implement so you can hit the ground running.

 This symbol shows a "bright idea" for you to consider as you start your business.

 This symbol indicates an interview tip for you. There's a whole chapter on interviewing so you ask the right questions to get the "straight scoop."

CHAPTER 1

The Straight Scoop on Real Estate Sales

Will You Love This Career?

"I learned more in real estate the first year about people and life than I ever learned in the formal education setting."

~Connie Kruse, top producer, formerly Dean of Business and Technology at a community college, and International Rookie of the Year for an international real estate franchise.

In This Chapter

- Why go into Real Estate Sales?
- Is This Career for You?
- Qualities and Strengths of the Successful Real Estate Agent
- Evaluation: Your Strengths—a Fit for Real Estate Sales?
- Behavioral Profiles and What They Mean to You
- Summary and Big Ideas
- Get a Jumpstart to Success

Why Go into Real Estate Sales?

In a recent survey by a major real estate company, agents were asked *why* they went into real estate. They answered:

- To be their own bosses
- For the freedom
- Because they like people
- To be different
- To meet new challenges

What's your reason: your big "why"? For many people, selling real estate offers a career of almost unlimited income potential and challenge. In fact, real estate is one of the last frontiers of business opportunity in the United States. One can get into real estate sales easily, with few educational requirements, and little cash outlay.

The Revolving Door: Why Are They Out of the Business Before Success?

If it's such a wonderful career, why do many agents go into and out of the business each year?

Another "10" on that honesty scale: Although no hard figures are available, my observation is that at least one-third to one-half of the licensees who start in the business each year fail to make it through one year. However, it takes two to three years to build a career that pays the dividends agents expect. Simply, many agents just don't commit to the number of years required to build a solid business. If they don't make lots of money in their first few months, they give up.

10 Statistics About Real Estate

1. 65% of REALTORS® are women.
2. 31% of REALTORS® have completed a bachelor's degree or higher.

3. The typical Realtor® is a 54-year-old white female who attended college and is a homeowner.

4. The median income for all REALTORS® is $43,300.

5. The typical Realtor® receives 34% of his business from repeat clients and referrals.

6. Increases in time in the business is reflected in more referrals: The agent with 16+ years in the business earns 59% of their business from repeat and referrals. The median number of transactions completed for all REALTORS® is ten.

7. 26% have had their license for two years or less.

8. 73% of REALTORS® specialize in residential real estate.

9. Income increases with numbers of years in the business. An agent with 16+ years in the business earns a median gross income of $75,000.

10. Hours worked: The agent working less than 20 hours has a median gross income of $9,800. The agent working 60+ hours has a median gross income of $99,000.

You Probably Don't Want to Become Some of these Statistics!

Why do some people earn low amounts of income—or fail? Some people just should not have gone into the business because they simply aren't cut out to be salespeople. They don't like doing the activities that assure success. They think real estate is an easy business requiring few hours and little effort. They reject the principles of sales generation, thinking there's a better way.

Is This the Right Career for You?

You have just bought a home. You enjoyed working with a real estate agent. Coincidentally, disenchanted with your position as a sales representative for a national company, you start thinking about real estate sales as a career alternative.

Like you, thousands of people each year consider real estate sales as a career change. Frequently, their outside-in view of real estate sales leads them to charge full force into the field and find out later that what they thought they were getting wasn't what they got! So that you can avoid leaping before you look, here is a way to see if your ideal job is real estate sales.

In this chapter, questionnaires focusing on YOU will help you search for strengths within yourself and create a futuristic picture of yourself in real estate. You'll see the characteristics and skills that successful real estate agents demonstrate. That way, you can decide whether:

- Your ideal job and real estate sales are a match
- You have the strengths that successful salespeople demonstrate in their real estate careers
- You'll like doing the tasks that successful agents do to create a stunningly successful real estate careers
- You have or are willing to acquire the skills needed for a successful career

Fig. 1.1   Your Ideal Job

Hours

☐ Regular hours (No weekends or nights; you like time restrictions.)

☐ Irregular hours (Like to finish a project; will work weekends, nights, if needed.)

Number of hours willing to work per week: _____

Time Frame

☐ Regular days off and vacation

☐ You name your schedule (Could work 14 days in a row, if needed, to accomplish a goal?)

Amount of Independence

☐ Supervised work with task completion expectations

☐ Unsupervised work; little evaluation or feedback from management

Salary

☐ Steady increase based on cost of living

☐ No salary (Your work determines your income)

Risk/Security

☐ Low risk (Job security)

☐ High risk (No guaranteed income, but low risk of getting "fired")

Comfort

☐ Little interference with private life

☐ Private life can be put on hold to achieve a goal

Working tasks or People

☐ Like working on tasks

☐ Like working with people

Work Environment

☐ Working with a group or in group activities

☐ Willing to work alone (like to be self-directed)

Planning

☐ Like a plan worked out for you

☐ Make your own plan to achieve goals or investment you may need to get into the profession

I've put an * besides the description of a real estate career. Compare your answers to the benefits and demands of being in business for yourself.

What's Your Ideal Job?

Let's start here. Use the categories in Fig. 1.1 to describe your ideal job. At this point, do not consider income.

Benefits of a Real Estate Career

Independence: Real estate salespeople are really on their own. They create their own weekly schedules, find business, market themselves, and budget their expenses. In fact, the best way to look at real estate careers is to consider that you are starting your own business under the "umbrella" of a real estate company.

People who have planned, organized, budgeted for, and managed other businesses find the skills they have developed in their previous businesses are directly transferable to real estate.

Have you had previous experience in business planning, budgeting, and management (including self-management)? Are you good at creating a prioritized work schedule and motivating yourself to follow through?

High Earning Capability: Real estate agents can earn large incomes through persistent hard work, patiently building their careers over a period of years.

Are you willing to work the number of hours it takes to be successful—and to do the business start-up plan of a successful agent? This isn't a job where you can work a couple of hours when it's convenient. If you want to make an attractive income, you must treat it like a real job.

Are you willing to sacrifice personal/family time at the beginning of your career to assure you generate income?

Low Barrier of Entry: Real estate sales requires a relatively small initial investment. One can get into the field quickly. So, it's an attractive alternative to buying a business franchise, or going to school to prepare to enter a profession.

Expenses start immediately. Income does not. The income stream builds up throughout the first year, as the new agent's expenses continue.

Typical Entry-Level Education: High school diploma or equivalent.

Opportunity for Career Advancement: Some real estate salespeople make more money in sales than managers and owners. As you develop your career, you may investigate opportunities to leverage your business systems, go into management, become a trainer or marketer, as well as the opportunity to own your own company.

Do the attractive attributes of real estate match your ideal career? Do the considerations within this discussion give you a better idea of the meaning behind the words? By being honest with yourself about these considerations, you can make a better career decision.

The Profile of a Successful Salesperson

There's probably no field more individualized than real estate sales. There are as many approaches to the business as there are people in the business. Yet, there are certain strengths that are common to successful salespeople. To know whether your strengths match those of successful salespeople, complete the self-inventory in Fig. 1.2.

Fig. 1.2   Self-Analysis: Attributes for Success

Rate yourself a 3 if you feel this particular attribute is a real strength of yours; 2 if you feel you're adequate; and 1 if you feel it's not one of your best qualities.

1. I do things on my own; nobody has to tell me to get going.   _____

2. I finish what I start, even if it takes me more time and effort than I thought it would.   _____

3. I'll tackle the challenging activities fast—I like to put myself in the action.   _____

4. I'm the one who plans the get-together; people look to me to organize activities.   _____

Fig. 1.2   Self-Analysis: Attributes for Success (cont'd)

5. I have accomplished things that others said I
   couldn't do; I knew I could.   _____

6. People depend on me because I follow
   through on a promise.   _____

7. I learn from others I respect; I put that
   information to use quickly.   _____

8. I get excited about accomplishing something;
   and this causes me to keep going.   _____

9. I can handle rejection without becoming
   devastated, because I know it's not personal.   _____

10. I've created ways to do things, and have done
    them, even when I didn't have lots of information.   _____

After you've rated yourself, read the qualities of successful real estate people, (figure 1.3), and compare them with your ratings.

Fig. 1.3   Qualities of a Successful Real Estate Agent Associate

High Personal Initiative
Your success depends on you being able to create programs, and implement them on your own, with relatively little monitoring.

Tenacity
Only those who stick with it will win. Plan on dedicating one year to establishing your business.

Mental Toughness
A positive mental attitude is essential. Those who give up easily will try to influence the tenacious, mentally tough individual to give up. It takes courage to keep going in this long-term business.

Fig. 1.3   Qualities of a Successful Real Estate Agent Associate (cont'd)

Belief in Oneself

We each have to know, inside ourselves, that we are capable, that we have the talent and the tenacity to succeed and must be able to depend on ourselves.

Willingness to Take Direction

Real estate is a constantly changing field. Those who win learn new skills and apply them consistently.

Enthusiasm

A joy in doing and a desire to accomplish show themselves in an enthusiastic attitude.

Creativity

In today's marketing-oriented world, an agent must be creative enough to design programs where he or she stands out as valuable and different.

Educated and Communicative

Writing skills are a necessity today. Effective verbal communication is also important to success. Our customers and clients expect good communication skills.

Team Player

The preservation of office spirit and cooperation is very important. We are all more successful together.

Strengths of Successful Real Estate Salespeople

Here's a longer explanation of those strengths, along with examples of how successful agents demonstrate them.

High Personal Initiative: In a salaried job, someone gives you a schedule, expectations, and time frames. The manager checks your work to be sure you finished it with a certain level of quality. If you don't do the job to your boss's satisfaction, you are redirected, reprimanded, or fired. So, the discipline generally comes from the structures, the job requirements, and your boss. In real estate, you're your own boss, and you drive your business, or not!

In real estate your manager generally does not become involved in scheduling your activities, checking that you completed those activities, or evaluating your work. Successful salespeople become their own managers from the start. If you've never been responsible only to yourself for achievement, you may find the "freedom" of real estate daunting.

If you're considering real estate sales because you don't want to be "bossed around," think again. Although you won't be told what to do by someone else, you will have to be your *own* boss. That's much more difficult!

As a new agent, no one told me what to do. In fact, I had only a part-time manager. I was really independent. The manager's approach could be characterized by an old quasi rhyme:

> "Here's your desk and here's your phone, good luck,
> you're on your own. Any questions? Ask me."

Ha! I didn't even know the questions, much less the answers. Aside from an occasional office meeting, and one segment of scheduled floor time (answering telephone inquiries) I had no idea how to schedule my time, and really no idea of the activities to do to be successful. I certainly didn't have a business start-up plan. How would I? I had been a music major! When I started my real estate career, I'd never even *heard* of business plans.

I did what all new agents do with no plan. I came into the office and hung around. I watched the activities of the agents that spent lots of time in the office. When they left the office, it was to preview new listings. They prided themselves on knowing all the inventory, but they seldom showed homes to prospects, and they very seldom made sales.

After watching this go on for about a week, I decided their method of selling real estate wasn't very exciting, much less lucrative. I figured, to sell homes you had to show them to buyers, not just look at them yourself.

So, I found buyers and sold three homes that first month, even before I knew all the inventory. The people in my office were displeased. "How *dare* she sell something before she knows all the properties available?" I apologized and kept selling homes.

Note from a reviewer (a very successful twenty-year sales/owner veteran): "My first company reprimanded me for taking too many listings. They said it made the other agents look bad."

Later, I wondered why I had to know all the inventory to be qualified to sell a home. Who made *those* rules? (Beware of rule-makers in any office. They can inhibit you from *launching right in real estate*. They are probably following a "failed agent" job description.) If you do not have high personal initiative, you can get stuck hanging around the office following the advice of people who might be following a "slow start," "failed agent" job description and poor or no business plan.

Tenacity: No one will be checking with you to see if you call clients back. You will have to be your own boss and make yourself keep your promises and finish what you start. You must exhibit great tenacity and inner discipline in your work, both in lead generation and follow-up.

As you talk to people to get leads, you'll hear "no" many more times than "yes." The ability to bounce back and keep going until you reach the desired outcome is paramount to your success. I've observed how quickly new agents become disappointed in themselves. Successful salespeople remember that tenacity always wins. Real estate salespeople don't get paid for their time. They get paid for their results: selling homes and listing homes that sell. Are you tough enough to take "no" for an answer and keep going to finally get a "yes"? How long are you willing to fail to win?

Risk Taker: Agents who jump right in and start finding leads have a much better chance of making money before their savings run out. They tackle the biggest challenges fast because they are willing to take a risk, fail and learn. They have high enough confidence in themselves to be able to say, "I don't know, but I'll find out." They realize that confidence comes from a successful action, and that we learn from doing!

Real life story: Even though Tim wasn't exactly sure how to fill the blanks, he completed an offer to purchase his first week in the business. He had to make some corrections, and was a little embarrassed about it, but chalked it up to a learning experience. With this attitude, Tim sold fourteen homes in four months. In contrast, some agents wait to write an offer to purchase until they know everything about these agreements. However, by the time they feel comfortable, they've forgotten most of the information. Use it or lose it. (Studies show we retain only 10 percent of what we heard 3 days earlier.)

Forget about learning everything about everything before you start talking to people. You can't learn fast enough or retain enough to succeed that way.

No. I don't mean to bumble around making things up. Check with your designated broker or manager before doing or writing something you are unsure of. Then, do it!

Accountability to Yourself: Planning your week, working your plan, and measuring the results of your plan ensure your success. Agents quickly learn that managers really do leave agents alone to be independent (or to fail independently). Some agents spend the first weeks of their career trying to *figure out* what to do. Then they are *scared* to do it. They procrastinate, seeking comfort in organizational activities--busy work, or, as I call it in *Up and Running in Real Estate*, business support. Months with no results pass quickly. I have watched this pattern develop again and again.

Belief in Oneself: It may take you a week, a month, or several months, to sell your first home. Your belief in your ability to meet new challenges will tide you over when things go wrong much more than they go right.

(When we get to the section on choosing a successful business start-up plan, I'll show you how to accurately project your income from your activities so you'll know when you're on or off track.)

Another real-life story: Kathy was only 22 when she started selling real estate. I hired her as a new agent. It was challenging at first, as she learned how to dress and talk to assure older people she was trustworthy and competent. But Kathy's strong belief in herself carried her to great success. Another characteristic that made Kathy successful was that she gracefully let me take the lead in helping her develop her career. My observation: Those who come into the business and, after two weeks in the office, either reject all suggestions to develop their business, or fight with the suggestions, do not do well!

After three years in the business, Kathy attained recognition in the top ten percent of our 500-agent company! "When the going gets tough, the tough get going" characterizes Kathy and all successful real estate salespeople.

Reliability to Others: Have people told you that they *knew* they could always *rely* on you? Reliability is so important to real estate success. Your customers and clients will ask themselves, "Is he reliable?" "Can I trust her?" They will draw their conclusions by remembering whether you kept your promises—or not. Building trust and confidence with the public is a series of kept promises. Each may be small individually, but they add up to a value judgment about the individual. In a National Association of REALTORS® *Survey of Buyers and Sellers*, the public rated *trustworthiness* and *reputation* as the most important attributes consumers want in a real estate agent.

Willingness to Learn: When you start something new, do you argue with the person teaching you about how to do it? Do you resist new ideas? Do you critique every idea? Do you resist getting into action? If so, look carefully at entering real estate. It's a *performance* business, not a *knowledge* endeavor. What is needed is willingness to consider an idea, while reserving judgment, and try it out.

Getting excited about an idea is the best short-term motivation for the new agent. When I interview a potential agent and find that I'm not sure which one of us is asleep, I question the person's short-term motivation to get into the business. Enthusiasm helps us throw ourselves into the task, to look at challenges as possibilities, to accept not knowing everything and just *do* something.

Able to Handle Rejection: Sales is a business where "no" is heard more than "yes." Our ability to accept "no," and keep going is key to sales success. Most people in sales give up too easily. An AT&T survey of their salespeople found that more than 90 percent of salespeople gave up after four "nos." But 80 percent of prospective buyers say "no" five times before they say "yes." So, one salesman out of ten makes 80 percent of the sales!

Creativity: This decade is an era of constant change, of turbulent markets, and increased competition. To stay ahead of the game, agents must keep changing and creating new sales strategies. I don't mean that you must be a creative marketing genius. Merely have fun with new ideas and implement some of them to ensure your success. Poor agents look for the *one* way that is guaranteed to always work. They spend their time judging others, not doing.

Skills Needed to Succeed Now

We have investigated the strengths that successful real estate agents exhibit. In addition, there are also three specific skills that are needed today to succeed at a high level.

 Remember how many times 'buyers' say 'no' when you start selling, so you won't get depressed with dozens of "nos."

Sales and Presentation Skills: In earlier decades, real estate salespeople relied almost solely on maintaining social relationships with their clientele to create business, and the real estate market took care of the rest. Now, with more sophisticated consumers and competitive salespeople, maintaining social relationships is not enough. Consumers expect salespeople to be businesspeople. They expect the agent to give them all the information in an organized, prioritized manner. The salesperson must learn to do this, even if it threatens the social relationship.

Never Give Up!

48% of salespeople give up after one call (one 'no')

Another 25% give up after 2 calls

Additional 12% give up after 3 calls

A hardy 5% give up after 4 calls

But, 80% of all sales are made after the 5th call!

Ability to Systematize. Historically, real estate sales has been a person-to-person business. Agents did it 'by ear'—that is, they operated by feel and instinct, without replicable systems. Now, it is impossible to create a reliable real estate business without developing the systems to support it. Growing your business with an assistant and/or a team requires those systems in place first.

Telling the Truth Attractively

You've developed sales skills and written a sales presentation to verify your point of view as fact, not opinion. You realize you owe it to your friend to *tell the truth attractively*, because you know overpriced homes sell for less than they are worth. So, you show the seller the market trends and explain how marketing and pricing work in the world of business. You realize that, to keep your friend's best interests in mind, you must put your business relationship before your friendship.

From reviewer Don Crawley, who brings humanity into the world of technology:

"Putting your business relationship first will ultimately protect your friendship."

Computer/Technology Skills: The most efficient real estate agents have enough computer skills that they can get what they need quickly. They can organize and run their business with systems, and they can market and use social media effectively. They're eager to learn new skills and realize they will keep adding to those skills throughout their careers.

Business Planning and Organizational Skills: Today, developing checklists and systems for effective business management is important. The business has become too complex for an agent to "wing it."

I learned this the hard way. As a new agent, I had no checklists to follow. So, I didn't know what to do when I sold a home. I didn't know I was supposed to remove the key box, call the listing office, or place a SOLD sign on the property. Boy, did I get nasty messages from my manager and the other office! After that, I started developing checklists and systems for every set of processes.

Today, successful agents use these operational guides for every conceivable activity set. Then, they can delegate many of these responsibilities to assistants, buyers' and sellers' agents, and other team members. They think of themselves as franchisors with the systems to duplicate their franchise even to other real estate markets. This is called "expansion", and successful agents are using this concept to build very successful companies-within-companies while duplicating them across the nation.

Most Important Factors in Choosing a Real Estate Agent

Take a look at this chart from the National Association of REALTORS® on important factors when choosing a real estate agent. Good news! What the public values do not have much to do with the experience level of the agent.

If you love computers more than you like people, watch out. This is a "people business" supported by relevant technology. Very few pure "techies" do well in this business.

In almost all instances, new agents can possess these, as well as seasoned agents. (Only two percent of the public put a high value on the agent's affiliation with a particular firm). In other words, just a firm name won't overcome poor performance! Remember that when you're interviewing. Here's another "ten":

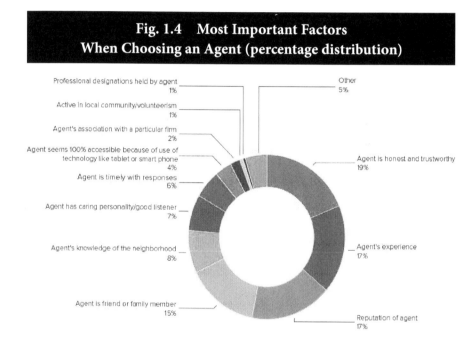

Fig. 1.4   Most Important Factors When Choosing an Agent (percentage distribution)

Professional designations held by agent — 1%
Active in local community/volunteerism — 1%
Agent's association with a particular firm — 2%
Agent seems 100% accessible because of use of technology like tablet or smart phone — 4%
Agent is timely with responses — 6%
Agent has caring personality/good listener — 7%
Agent's knowledge of the neighborhood — 8%
Agent is friend or family member — 15%
Other — 5%
Agent is honest and trustworthy — 19%
Agent's experience — 17%
Reputation of agent — 17%

A Top Producer's Behaviors

Why do some people make a success of something, while others, seemingly as talented, fail? It's not about their credentials, or what they are. It is about what they *do*. Here's a study of top producers through the activities they complete. A University of Illinois study found that top producers:

- Were self-starters and had high energy
- Worked more days, evenings, and weekends than average producers

- Were intensely task-oriented
- Took part in relatively little social conversation on the job
- Completed more face-to-face contacts
- Had high standards for prospects (qualified them stringently before they would put buyers in the car or go to listing presentations)
- Had high client candor (frankly told them the truth, even if the client didn't want to hear it)
- Needed recognition more than security (the only one of the profile not an action item)

Good News for New Agents: Researchers have found that experience beyond one year was an insignificant factor to high productivity. This means it's possible to build a dynamic career in real estate quickly if you demonstrate the behaviors in this study of top producers.

Behavioral Profiling Tools: Match your Strengths to Real Estate Sales

Businesses have used assessment tools to match the right people to the right jobs for years. These tools are termed "behavioral assessments," or "behavioral profiles." They measure how different types of people behave naturally. They track what these types of people like to do and feel comfortable doing. Psychologists have concluded, through exhaustive studies, that certain types of people generally gravitate to, and are successful at, certain types of jobs.

Tasks vs. People

For instance, some people like to work on tasks. To them, a checklist of tasks to complete is heaven-sent. These people become accountants, computer experts, and office managers. To others, the thought of sitting at a computer doing data-entry every day would be hell! Instead, they love to work with people.

Recently, I was talking with a man who was exploring a career in real estate sales. He said, "I go to many open houses and evaluate them.

I really enjoy that." I asked him what he had done for a living in the past. He told me he was an accountant. Do accountants deal mainly with tasks or with people? Tasks. What do you think this would-be agent will focus on? How successful will he be?

Since real estate success depends on helping *people* achieve their goals in the home buying and selling process, people-oriented people enjoy by far the most success.

Dozens of these behavioral tools are available, from inexpensive 15-minute assessments to those that take hours and cost hundreds of dollars. More and more real estate companies and agents are using these assessment tools to match the right people to the right jobs. These tools are used by mega-agents to match applicants to their team job descriptions, by owners to match managers to their job descriptions, and by managers to match agents to their job descriptions.

One inexpensive and accurate behavioral profiling tool is the DISC (see www.Abelson.net for more information and great interpretations). I like the Abelson version because there is a version expressly for real estate positions that has realistic, thorough interpretations. These tools are likely to take on greater importance in real estate, so companies make fewer hiring mistakes, and would-be agents avoid getting into a sales field when they should be in a task-oriented position.

From the company's perspective, it costs from $10,000 to $30,000 to support a new agent in the first six months! That's a huge investment, and one that takes two to three years to recover, per agent. So, if the agent fails, the company has just lost its investment, which affects profitability. How much would it cost you as an agent to fail? Too much to leave the selection and match-up to a "gut feeling."

How to Take Advantage of Behavioral Profiles: As you interview, take advantage of opportunities to complete a behavioral profile. Hopefully, you will receive a professional interpretation. Ask the manager to take at least one-half hour to share the results, discuss what the results mean, and match those results with the job description in Chapter two. The manager should be able to alert you to your strengths that match those

Getting into and staying in a job you don't like leads to stress, which leads to avoidance of the tasks required in the job.

required in real estate sales, and to discuss with you the challenges you will face.

Knowing vs. Doing

While it's true that one can be trained to do most anything, it's also true that we do what we really *want* to do with our time, and what we are naturally "wired" to do long-term. When we force ourselves to take actions we don't want to take, we become stressed. That's why we get out of those jobs we didn't like. Don't go jumping out of the frying pan into the fire. Match your behavioral profile to the prioritized job description of a successful real estate agent, as I've shared in this book.

Behavioral Profiles and the Jobs People Choose with Those Profiles

Read quotes of a group of managers discussing the type of people they like and don't like to hire:

- "I love teachers. They're so helpful and they're great communicators."
- "Beware of hiring someone who's retired military. They're used to structure and telling others what to do."
- "I don't hire any new agents I need to train. I like to hire only experienced agents."
- "I never hire people unless they've worked at least three different jobs."

Every manager has his or her preferences. Generally, managers hire people like themselves. Everyone brings the pluses and minuses from their earlier life experiences to real estate sales. Also, what you did before and how you did it and what you like doing in the job greatly influences how you'll go about creating your "version" of a real estate career. Looking at backgrounds can reveal how these influences help and challenge one's chances of real estate success.

Most behavioral profile tools separate behavioral styles into four "quadrants" or more (Fig. 1.5). I'm describing each of these quadrants here.

As I describe these profiles, I suggest how each profile must "move" on a behavioral continuum. I don't mean you must become someone else. Instead, have *the flexibility* to flex your style to meet the situation. Many behavioral profiles measure a person's ability to flex.

Fig. 1.5 Behavioral Profiles	
Analyticals	**Controllers**
Job preferences:	Job preferences:
Accountants	CEO
Engineers	Military
Task-based jobs	In-charge jobs
Nurturers	**Promoters**
Job preferences:	Job preferences:
Nurses	Sales
Teachers	Show business
Administrative staff	Persuasive jobs

Behavioral profiles are variations of these and many other qualities. They can vary between how one perceives himself and how he perceives others see him. I have simplified the information to give readers an overview of how behavioral profiling can help guide you to the right career decision. People are actually *some combination* of all of the quadrants, and people exhibit relative strengths in these quadrants.

Nurturers (Examples: Teachers, Social Workers, and Home Managers): These people went into these professions because they enjoy helping people. With that attitude, they can be a success in real estate. But watch out. They may be willing to knock on doors for a good cause, but are they willing to ask people to buy? Are they tough enough to handle sales rejection? Are they tough enough to take six "no's" to get a "yes"? Frequently, people from these fields find that they get walked all over, and then they either get tough or get out of the business.

A nurturer doesn't want the word "salesperson" on business cards, and fears that people won't like them if they know they want to sell them something. Nurturers do not like the connotations they ascribe to the word "salesperson."

To get over this, nurturers must convince themselves that sales is a valuable *service*. They must convince themselves too that it is in the customer's best interest to work with them because of their nurturing traits. Nurturers also need to keep their eyes on the goal—selling the home. They can get lost in service to people and forget to finish the task. Nurturers need to find a supportive, firm environment with a manager who understands their strengths and needs one who will lovingly push them out the door. "Tough love" works here.

For nurturers to succeed, they must be able to flex their style:

- From empathy to ego (think more of themselves and less of others)
- From people to tasks (focus more on getting the job done).

When you put successful real estate agents in a room, only about 5 percent of them would be termed "nurturers." Why? Nurturers tend not to be tough enough to take rejection. They hate lead generating. They are so "people pleasing" that they would give up a commission to make the seller happy (not exactly a win-win situation!). They don't have enough ego drive to persevere to a "close."

Nurturers' Motto: "I just LOVE supporting people."

Controllers (Examples: Managers, Attorneys, Retired Military People Who Have Been in Positions of Authority): Controllers like to tell people what to do and expect them to do it! With that take-charge attitude, they can do well in real estate sales. They have no trouble telling people to buy. They just order them to do it fast. And if the customer doesn't buy, they get frustrated. So, they must learn to back off. In real estate sales, they are no longer the boss. Now, there is much less structure to hang onto and to hold others to. They must develop several latent qualities; one is patience.

A fellow in our office who owned several companies and took early retirement is a controller. He liked to cut right to the chase and close, but he couldn't figure out why some of his clients didn't do as he said. In fact, he lost clients because they said he was pushy.

When I went into real estate and found I had so much to learn, I felt out of control. I got angry and frustrated; I lost patience; I came home at night, yelled at my family, and threw pots and pans. I hated not knowing all the answers. I always felt embarrassed. My most used phrase seemed to be, "I don't know, but I'll find out."

The only way I learned a little patience was that I became fascinated with sales and with the ability to "control" a sales situation (my nickname was "the velvet sledgehammer"). Controllers who slow down and consider their customer's needs find that the game of sales becomes *fun*. They are in control, but much more subtly than before.

Controllers: The Manager you Need. To succeed, a controller needs a manager who sets firm guidelines, lays out a simple plan, and gives lots of praise for results. A last word from one controller to another: become childlike. Look at it as a new adventure. As a "babe in the woods," you can enhance some of your other qualities you need to redevelop to be successful in your new career.

For controllers to succeed in real estate sales, they must flex their style:

- From ego to empathy (pay more attention to customers/ clients)
- From tasks to people (pace the flow of the sales process to your customer's needs).

In a room full of real estate agents, about 45 percent will be controllers. Only about ten percent, by the way, are a combination of controller and promoter. The bad news is that, without strong management, the controller can run amuck, bullying managers and less aggressive agents. When you're new, look for a company whose embraced value system is win-win, and whose guidelines stop highly aggressive, successful salespeople from running all over new agents and clients.

Controllers' Motto: "I tell 'em what to do and expect them to do it."

Promoters (Examples: Marketers, Salespeople): They have it *all*, right? They are good talkers, they're flashy, they're outgoing—the epitome of the salesperson. It's true that people in sales and promotion have valuable traits and skills. They intuitively understand the sales process, and characteristically have a great personality—they love people! They can be great successes in real estate sales, but they also have challenges. They love people *so* much that they don't want to tell them bad news. They *hate* rejection and take it personally.

Promoters must learn to give bad news and be able to risk rejection. Otherwise, promoters get known as slippery salespeople! Also, promoters have trouble finishing tasks. Why? They would rather be with the *people*.

"Sally should go into real estate. She's a good talker." I hear people suggest that regularly. But sales requires excellent *listening skills*, not talking skills, especially today. Clients don't want to be *talked into* buying. They want information, counseling, and help with the decision-making process. They want to be listened to. Some of the best salespeople I have ever known are the quietest.

Promoters: The Manager You Need. Find a manager you can talk to. Promoters need a reasonable structure to form their day and keep them on track. They need enough support to withstand rejection and do the hard things, such as taking "no" and giving out the bad news.

For promoters to succeed in real estate sales, they flex their style:

- From empathy to ego (toughen up to take rejection)
- From people to tasks (don't get diverted from the goal).

Back to the room full of real estate salespeople: About 45 percent will be promoters. If they have enough task orientation, they will be successful.

Motto: "I have the gift of gab and can convince anyone of anything."

Analyticals (Examples: Accountants, Engineers): Years ago, people who liked tasks more than people were discouraged from going into sales. But, with the technical knowledge required today, the increased paperwork load, and the attention to detail needed to provide good customer service, the task-oriented person can do well in real estate if they have at least some "people" orientation. They also have challenges. Because they tend to look at real estate sales as tasks to be completed, task-oriented people will grasp a list of tasks and continue doing them even if they're not getting results. They forget that the goal is to help clients make buying decisions, which in turn culminate in commissions to the agent. They must be helped to analyze the list of tasks, to measure results, and revise the task list to ensure results. Most importantly, they must develop people skills.

For most of their lives, analyticals have gotten results by doing the task. It is difficult for them to focus on the people. So, they must think about the sales process as a group of tasks that involves people. Otherwise, they will hide in the paperwork, filing, collating, and recording. To get out of that rut, they will have to be self-motivated. Their biggest challenge in sales is that they hate lead generating.

The Manager an Analytical Needs. A task-oriented person needs to find a manager who will provide a detailed, proven business-producing plan, and who will work closely with the new agent to monitor and analyze activities and results and keep the agent on track, while providing training to develop sales skills. That way, the task-oriented person can realize monetary results and avoid doing tasks that do not lead to results.

For task-oriented people to succeed in real estate sales, they must flex their style:

- From ego to empathy (learn to consider the differences in people)
- From tasks to people.

In that room of successful agents, only about five percent are Analytical. Why? Because the true analytical doesn't have enough desire to work with people to enjoy the people-oriented sales process, especially face-to-face lead generating. The analytical distrusts "salespeople" and so has trouble helping buyers and sellers make decisions quickly.

Analyticals' Motto: "I love houses. I just hate people."

Summary

In your interview, ask the manager how he or she would manage to your behavioral style. A good manager acts as a business consultant to you, using the coaching and consulting skills and tools the manager has developed over the years to benefit your career growth.

There are many misconceptions about real estate sales. As a commissioned salesperson, you are in charge of your budget, your expenses, your income—and your profits. You are really the owner of your own business.

Big Ideas in this Chapter

- Before you leap into real estate sales, take the time to match your strengths, goals, and expectations with those expressed in this chapter.
- Successful real estate agents exhibit common skills and talents.
- Certain behavioral profiles tend to succeed in real estate.

If one is in a business or tries to force herself into an activity she doesn't want to do, she will put herself under stress. Taking the time to assess your profile before you launch into a real estate career will help you succeed at whatever you do.

Get a Jump-Start on Success

- Use figure 1.1, Your Ideal Job, to see whether real estate sales may be a 'fit' for you.

- Use the self-analysis tool, figure 1.2, to assess your strengths and talents. Compare that with the profile of the successful real estate salesperson, figure 1.3.

- Behavioral profiles: Which of these profile quadrants best reflects you? Take a comprehensive behavioral profile to see if your strengths and profile match those of a successful real estate agent.

CHAPTER 2

What a Real Estate Agent Does to Make Money Fast

"Pick up the phone. I recommend getting scripts and practicing over and over until it's natural to you."

~ Raymond Megie, chosen for the "Top 30 under 30" feature article (top REALTORS® under 30 years of age) in the *National Association of REALTORS® Magazine*, and No. 1 agent in his local Board of REALTORS®

- In This Chapter
- Busy Work vs. Income-Producing Work
- Your Successful Agent Prioritized Job Description
- The Business Start-Up Plan to Make Money Now
- How Selling Real Estate is Different from Other Sales
- Real Estate as your First Career
- Working with your Spouse/Partnerships
- Big Ideas
- Get a Jump-Start to Success

How do real estate agents make money? Before I tell you, here's a question. Do you want to make money right away, or would you prefer waiting months to get your first check?

That's not a facetious question. It's a real one. It's possible to make money fast in this business. It's possible to make money slowly. In this chapter, we will investigate the activities real estate agents do to make money. I'll also provide a prioritized job description for a successful real estate agent. Agents who make money fast use this *prioritized* job description.

"Busy Work" vs. "Income-Producing Work": Unfortunately, when you interview at a real estate company, you probably won't receive a job description for your position. Hearing the sales presentation, you may conclude the job is different than it really is. Let's work through the steps to create a job description for a *successful* real estate agent—successful in the *first year*.

An agent can take part in literally dozens of activities during a business week, such as:

- Preview your office's new listings on an office tour
- Preview properties listed by other agencies
- Complete paperwork on transactions
- Create virtual tours
- Create a virtual listing presentation
- Create a virtual buyer presentation
- Follow up with clients
- Follow up with prospects
- Set showing appointments
- Engage in social media
- Do research on the Internet
- Show properties to buyers
- Attend office meetings, both live and virtual
- Attend educational sessions

- Attend Realtor® meetings/committee work
- Find potential clients
- Do listing presentations
- Learn about title, escrow, finance, and closing procedures
- Organize materials/your desk
- Answer calls at an office on a schedule assigned by office personnel (commonly called floor time)
- Hold open houses for the public
- Hold open houses for the cooperating agents (brokers' opens)
- Prepare paper and virtual brochures for properties
- Promote yourself (preparing brochures, cards, etc., to distribute to identified markets, or other promotions to increase name recognition)
- Follow up on transactions to the end of the transaction (closings—getting paid)
- Study finance options
- Plan your days, weeks, and long-term goals

Some of these activities produce income. Many of them don't. Those activities that don't directly produce income are called "support work". However, the support work (or "busy work") takes up time and, for some people, it's preferable to the income-producing work. Why? Because finding and working with real people is more challenging than doing "get ready" or support work. As new agents quickly learn, the array of activities one can do seems endless. And, if these activities aren't prioritized into an effective business start-up plan, the result is no income.

Job Descriptions: Prioritized or Not?

Below: An actual job description (Figure 2.1) that one manager provides his candidates (interviewees). (I haven't changed any of the wording or phrasing). As you read it, ask yourself this question: How successful do you think a real estate agent would be if she followed this job description?

Successful salespeople spend much more time in business-developing activities.

Unsuccessful salespeople spend more time in business-maintenance activities.

Fig. 2.1   Job Description for a Licensed Real Estate Agent (not Carla's)

Establish, with your manager's help, your professional (sales) goals for the running year, including monthly, weekly and daily goals, and set up how to achieve them.

Know the company's marketing area: its geography, demographics, socioeconomic factors, neighborhood characteristics, schools, stores, transportation and recreation facilities.

Know the inventory (of residential properties for sale). Be thoroughly familiar with the listings of this office. Know the company's listing. Be familiar with the listings of our multiple listing system.

Hold floor time (or "Up Time") or equivalent. Serve regularly scheduled periods in the office to: (a) answer incoming phone calls; (b) serve walk-in customers; (c) take messages for out-of-office agents.

Get listings. Fill out exclusive listing agreement; get it signed by seller.

Show and sell property. Earnest money properly completed, signed. submitted to seller, and accepted and signed by seller.

Go on tours ("caravans").

Attend all scheduled meetings.

Follow-up all transactions (paperwork, phone calls etc.)

Fig. 2.1   Job Description for a Licensed Real Estate Agent (not Carla's) (cont'd)

Appraise property.

Maintain all forms, sales tools. etc.

Meet "continuing education" (clock hour) requirements and maintain professional development.

Favorably represent the company.

Maintain personal appearance compatible with your market and reflecting favorably the image of the company.

Maintain your car/a car. Maintain in safe. clean and comfortable condition a car of such type, make and class as to reflect favorably on the company and the agent.

Maintain a steady flow of prospective clients/customers through referrals, prospecting, etc.

Know (and follow) Office Procedures

There's Dangerous 'Safety' in Certain Activities

Which of the activities above do you believe a new real estate agent will do easily and willingly? Which activities are 'safe' (no rejection and/or no sales skills required?) Which activities will be challenging? What kind of schedule do you believe a new agent will make if given this kind of job description? How much money do you think that new agent will make—and when?

Business-Producing vs. Business Support Activities

Earlier, I called some 'get ready' activities "busy work". To clearly differentiate between the type of activities we do, I've created two categories: Business-supporting activities (busy work or get ready work) and business producing work—the activities that lead to a check.

Note from reviewer: Rhyme that portrays the person stuck in business support-- "One for the money, two for the show, three to get ready, three to get ready, three to get ready...."

Your Turn to Prioritize

Go back and mark the job description above activities as BP (business producing) vs. BS (business-supporting). Which is the bigger list?

Write Your Job Description

What are the activities that lead to income? (Hint: If you didn't do these activities, would you make money?)

What are the activities that are support or busy work? (Hint: If you did all of these, but didn't do the activities in category one, would you make money?)

This is your job description, prioritized so you are focused on creating income. As you begin your career, keep this job description in a prominent area so you train your brain to think through your business like a top producer.

The Successful Real Estate Agent's Prioritized Job Description

Fig. 2.2 is my prioritized job description for a successful agent. Compare it to any job descriptions you may have gotten (or that you just created). Be sure your job description is prioritized, based on the activities that actually make you money!

**Fig. 2.2   Prioritized Job Description for a Successful
Real Estate Salesperson**

Three categories of activities that our agents consistently perform to become successful fast.

1. Develop and implement a business plan
   - Find potential customers and clients by identifying target markets
   - Lead generate to find buyers and sellers daily and in great numbers

     Skills required: Lead generation, Marketing, Sales
     Traits required: Aggression, Tenacity, Self-Starter

     Our agents' income and quick success are largely determined by the number of people contacted regularly (lead generation)

2. Sales activities generated as result of a business plan
   - Showing homes to qualified customers
   - Selling homes
   - Listing marketable properties to sell in normal market time

     Skills required: Sales, marketing
     Traits required: Tenacity

3. Activities that assure a check
   - Selling homes that close
   - Listings sold that close

**Fig. 2.2   Prioritized Job Description for a Successful
Real Estate Salesperson (cont'd)**

4. Other activities
   - Preparation and support activities
   - Preview properties
   - Paperwork/sales follow up
   - Education
   - Meetings

   *Doing too many activities in the last category without doing the
   activities in the first three categories in great numbers assures failure.*

Now, let's put some numbers next to the critical income-creating activities, so we create a business start-up plan for you.

Your Best Business Start-up Plan

There is no magic bullet for success. Well, I was wrong. There *is* a magic bullet, and it is figure 2.3. This is what to do your first year in the business to launch a very successful career.

Fig. 2.3   Your Best Business Start-Up Plan

Goal of this business plan: Sell 12 homes your first year.

- Lead generate to find buyers and sellers (50 to 100 per week)
- Qualify buyers and sellers (two buyers per week/one seller per week)
- Show homes to qulified buyers (two showings per week)
- List salable properties (one or two per month)
- Sell properties (one to two per month)

This plan will deliver one to two transactions per month.

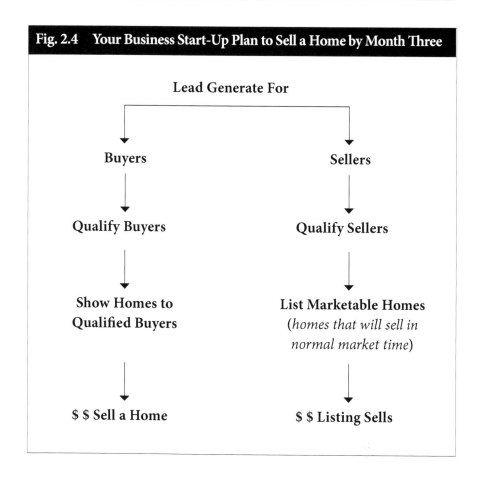

Fig. 2.4   Your Business Start-Up Plan to Sell a Home by Month Three

Lead Generate For

Buyers

Sellers

Qualify Buyers

Qualify Sellers

Show Homes to
Qualified Buyers

List Marketable Homes
(*homes that will sell in
normal market time*)

$ $ Sell a Home

$ $ Listing Sells

Your Business Path to Success

Figure 2.4 looks simple and it is. The challenge is that there are lots of support activities that seem to get in the way and take up time.

Complete Twelve Transactions in your First Year

As you interview, ask each manager for the company's prioritized job description and the business start-up plan you will be using as a new agent.

How Selling Real Estate is Different from other Sales

Maybe you have had another sales career in the past. Don't assume selling real estate will be the same. There are three major differences between real estate sales and other commissioned sales positions:

1. Real estate salespeople must go out and find leads—prospective sellers and buyers. Few prospects are given to the agents by management. This is one of the things to listen for in the interview. If the manager promises you leads, run, don't walk out of that office! Real estate managers today simply don't have the marketing money to spend to generate enough leads for new agents to make a living. And, commission splits are no longer 50/50 (that's where the money came from....). However, some managers entice naive agents to their offices by promising "good floor time" or "good open houses" or "great internet leads." If it were that easy, commissions certainly wouldn't be as generous as they are! You'll see more about that later in the Interview section.

2. Real estate salespeople cannot depend on media advertising (newspaper, TV, social media, etc.) to generate enough inbound calls to meet their income expectations (unless three to five sales a year are enough for you).

3. Unlike some sales businesses (pharmaceuticals or radio ad time sales) real estate salespeople have no assigned territory. You can sell anywhere; you must have the discipline to choose an area and work it consistently.

4. In general, generating prospects is almost solely up to the real estate salesperson. That is why the field enjoys almost unlimited earning potential, and why the commissions to the agent are so generous. Ironically, that is one reason why so many people fail in real estate in their first year. Not understanding the nature of the business, they sit and wait for prospects to come to them instead of going out to find them.

Ask the manager if she will assist you in creating your "lead generation" plan. Does she use a plan such as *Up and Running in 30 Days*?

Your plan should tell you how many sales calls you need to complete to earn a sale and should give you the specific sales dialogue to make the call. It should have prototype numbers to hit and a way to measure success

In the next few paragraphs, I'll answer some of the concerns and questions would-be agents frequently ask during their interviews.

Real Estate as Your First Career

As you graduate from high school or college, you may be considering real estate as a career. Is it a good career for a young person? More and more recent graduates have chosen real estate sales. Why? High income potential, ownership, and related investment opportunities. It is a good career choice if you are mature, capable of accepting lots of responsibility, and are willing to look at sales as a long-term commitment. The National Association of REALTORS® survey showed this was the first career for 5% of new REALTORS®.

There are certain things you can do to gain acceptance with clients. One is to dress conservatively. Another is to drive a conservative car and drive conservatively. Communicate that you are serious, understanding, and capable of helping people with the largest investment most people will ever make: a home. Young people bring lots of great qualities to real estate:

- Enthusiasm
- Energy (without it, you can't maintain the hours needed to launch your career)
- Creativity (being willing to try new things)
- Willing to take direction

- You also bring valuable skills to the business that many older real estate salespeople never gained
  - A better education than your predecessors
  - Knowledge of business planning and organizational skills
  - If you majored in business, sales and marketing knowledge
  - Technical and computer skills

 If you're in college now, see if you can do an apprenticeship with a real estate company. You'll learn the ins and outs of sales, observe the salespeople, and get a sense of what it's like to sell real estate. Don't justify because there's too much space between the words.

According to the National Association of REALTORS® member survey, 4% of REALTORS® are 30 years old or under. With the excellent educational and training programs available today, I strongly encourage young people to consider real estate sales seriously.

Working with Your Spouse

Husband-wife teams can be successful. It is another partnership. The key is to decide which duties each will perform before starting to work together. Read the description of behavioral styles. Which one are you? Which one is your spouse? Which real estate activities will each of you enjoy doing? Can you divide your duties to match your styles and strengths?

Strong, true partnerships work best when both agents run their individual businesses. They help each other in time crunches. Or one agent acts as the salesperson, and one agent is the assistant.

George and Martha Scott are both successful salespeople. They were in the business as individuals several years before they married. They co-list homes, telling sellers that they are getting *twice* the service for the same cost. However, to maximize their earnings, they sell homes individually. When one of them gets in a pinch, the other helps out. This arrangement works well because they really treat it as a true partnership. It also works because they both have a salesperson's behavioral profile.

Partnerships vs. salesperson and assistant. Frequently, this is what happens as a 'partnership' develops. One person sells while the other person does the paperwork. It is actually a salesperson working with an assistant. There is nothing wrong with this division of duties. However, the salesperson may believe he/she is worth more in the 'partnership' than the assistant.

Determining the arrangement. Here is a way to determine which kind of arrangement you should consider. If one of you enjoys paperwork, organization, and follow-up support activities, that person becomes the assistant. While teaching one of my business planning classes, I was impressed with a student, who was well organized, perceptive, and supportive (we instructors love these people!). She told me she was her husband's assistant and was there to get him organized! For some, that works.

My husband observed that I have organized and managed thousands of people, but in all our years of marriage, I haven't made any progress with him! (It took us years to recognize that fact and work together only in those areas we could keep from killing each other).

There is no right or wrong working arrangement. If you think any kind of spouse partnership is for you, find some people in selling

When you interview, ask managers their opinion about partnerships and how they handle them in their offices (desk space, commissions, etc.)

partnerships and in assistant partnerships. Ask them how they've made it a success.

Summary

In closing this chapter, finish your internal review by answering these questions:

- Do you see yourself more clearly now as a real estate salesperson? If so, in what ways?
- What strengths do you see demonstrated in your life that will assist you in real estate sales?
- What do you think will be your biggest challenges?
- What skills (sales, technical) do you need to learn? How will you learn them?
- What kind of office, management, and support systems will benefit you?

Save the information from the last two questions for your interview. You will want to ask interview questions to find the particular manager and office to help you optimize your strengths and meet your specific challenges.

Big Ideas from Chapter 2

- Having a correctly prioritized job description from the get-go to guide you is important to your short and long-term success.
- Without this job description. You will subconsciously choose the activities you like to do, rather than the ones that lead to a paycheck.

- Starting with a proven, prioritized start-up plan will save you thousands of dollars and will result in earlier success.
- Lead generating isn't a choice—it's an *absolute* for success.

 ### Get a Jump-Start on Success

- Create your prioritized job description. Compare it to any you receive as you interview.
- Make a list of 200+ people you know.
- Draft a letter to introduce yourself and let those people know you're in real estate (email or snail mail after you're licensed, of course).
- Create a business start-up plan and compare it to those you receive as you interview (if you receive any!).

CHAPTER 3

The Formula to Succeed Quickly

"Marketing and lead generation go hand in hand. Consistency, steadiness, follow up...repeat. It takes several touches to reach your goal of getting to a yes. Stay on task."

~ Craig Walker, top-producing first year agent, Bellevue, Wa.

In This Chapter

- How Much Time Does It Take?
- The Formula for Success
- The Schedule of a Successful New Agent
- Four Truths About Lead Generation You May Not Be Told
- A Day in the Life of a Successful Real Estate Agent
- Can I Have a Life?
- Gaining Support from your Family and Others
- How to Plan for After the "Newbie" Phase
- Big Ideas
- Get a Jump-Start to Success

How Much Time Does It Take?

After interviewing hundreds of potential agents, I can predict the most-asked questions. This is one of the most common: "How much time do I have to devote daily to become successful?"

Answer: As long as it takes!

Second Answer: At least 40 hours a week to build a career. It's a real job!

Unlike salaried positions, real estate agents are not paid for the number of hours on the job. They're paid for results. But, because most new agents come from salaried positions, where working the required number of hours ensured being retained, it's difficult for them to grasp the concept that to be successful in real estate, business-producing activities must be performed until the desired results are attained (even if it takes longer than the agent had planned).

What You Do Determines How Much You Make

It's not just how long you're on the job; it is what you do that determines your income. Think of this the way you think about remodeling your home. You start the project, estimating it will take three months. After three months, you're half-finished (I know, I lived through it). But, because your goal is a finished remodel, you continue the job until you get the result you want. You understand the concept. Still, what does this mean a new agent has to do each day to become successful? Approximately how long will it take a new agent to do it?

General Time Requirements

Even though time on the job doesn't guarantee success, some general time requirements are essential to create a successful career. According to the National Association of REALTORS®, a member works an average of 35 hours a week. (That's the average Realtor®, not the very successful one).

New agents need to plan on spending 45 to 50+ hours a week working their first year.

Why? Because it takes them longer to generate leads. It takes them longer to close a sale, because they are learning on the job to qualify and close.

Just as you would not want to stop in the middle of a fascinating project, will-be successful new agents find they love spending long hours establishing their careers. They want to conquer the challenges they face as new agents, and they are willing to devote the time necessary to establish a great career.

Even though the number of hours worked does not assure success, the fact is that longer hours equate to much more income. A Realtor® survey stated that REALTORS® who work fewer than 20 hours a week have a median gross personal income of $9,800, while a Realtor® who works more than 60 hours a week has a median gross personal income of $115,600. Here's another "10" on the honesty scale: You can't work a few hours a week—at your convenience—and expect to rake in the bucks!

The Quick-Start Formula

 The Pareto Principle applies to real estate sales: 20% of your activities will yield you 80% of your results. Where are you going to spend that 20%?

Chapter 2 contrasted all the activities agents can do in a business week with the critical, or essential, activities they must do to get a paycheck. ("Business producing" vs. "business supporting" activities). Look at these business-producing activities as a "sales path." Fig. 3.1 shows these business-producing activities agents do every day to start and journey on this sales path to success.

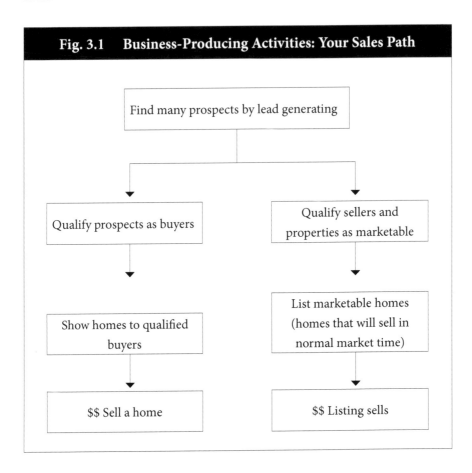

Fig. 3.1   Business-Producing Activities: Your Sales Path

Find many prospects by lead generating

Qualify prospects as buyers

Qualify sellers and properties as marketable

Show homes to qualified buyers

List marketable homes (homes that will sell in normal market time)

$$ Sell a home

$$ Listing sells

The formula: Stay on the sales path. Paths lead to destinations. When you wander off a path, you may find interesting diversions, but it takes longer to reach your destination (if you ever reach it!). When you stay on the business-producing sales path, doing these activities consistently, you can make money fast. The more business-supporting activities (Fig. 3.2) you complete while doing fewer business-producing activities, the less money you make in a given period of time. Yet, there are virtually hundreds of business-supporting activities agents can do to fill time. And they do. However, the principle of sales success follows the 80/20 rule: 20 percent of the activities you do will yield you 80 percent of the results. So, you must figure out that 20 percent, fast!

Don't Practice a Failed Business Plan: The most frightening part about getting off the business-producing activity path is that you'll be teaching yourself a job description and business plan that leads to failure, not success. You know how hard habits are to break! So many agents fail because they taught themselves a "business-supporting business plan"! Let's revisit my prioritized job description (fig.3.3).

Fig. 3.2   Business-supporting activities

- Education and meetings

- Organizing files

- Having coffee with the gang

- Creating mailers/other marketing

- Creating marketing tactics

- Previewing properties

- Learning technology

- Critiquing another's business

- Following up with transactions

- Marketing a listing (not face-to-face)

Fig. 3.3   Prioritized Job Description for a Successful Real Estate Salesperson

Three categories of activities that our associates consistently perform to become successful agents, to make money fast:

1. **Develop and implement a business plan:**
   * Find potential customers and clients by identifying target markets.
   * Prospect to find buyers and sellers daily and in great numbers.
      - **Skill required:** Prospecting, marketing, sales.
      - **Traits required:** Aggression, tenacity.

   Our agents' quick income and quick success are largely determined by the number of people contacted regularly (prospecting).

2. **Sales activities generated as result of a business plan:**
   * Showing homes to qualified customers.
   * Selling homes.
   * Listing marketable properties to sell in normal market time.
      - **Skills required:** Sales, marketing.
      - **Traits required:** Tenacity.

3. **Activities that assure a check:**
      - Selling homes that close.
      - Listings sold that close.

4. **Other activities:**
   * Preparation and support activities:
      - Preview properties.
      - Paperwork/sales follow-up.
      - Education.
      - Meetings.

Doing too many activities in the last category without doing the activities in the first three categories in great numbers assures failure.

How Are You Feeling About the Prioritized Job Description?

As you read the success formula, how are you feeling? Energized? Or, are you rejecting it and looking for a "better way"?

Margie interviewed with me for a sales position. I gave her our prioritized job description and asked her to review my book with the start-up plan, *Up and Running in 30 Days.* I explained that this business plan was the one we use to help new agents launch careers fast. At the same time, Margie was interviewing with another manager at another real estate company. That manager gave Margie no job description or start-up plan. However, she did offer Margie a sales position after ten minutes of talking with her. Margie was so thrilled to get hired she decided to work there. She felt more comfortable with the other manager because nothing would be asked of her. After a month, Margie called me. She complained, "There's no direction, no support, and no training. I'm failing. Help!" She found out that no expectations of her meant she could have no expectations of management.

What Happens Long-Term?

Most agents get out of the business within the first year when they don't get the immediate success they expect (see my survey in Appendix B). My observation: A few agents just keep tramping in the trenches. They finally begin making some money by their third or fourth year. Sadly, though, they have developed the habits for a low- or mid-producing career. Think what they could have accomplished with a great coach, a proven business start-up plan, and someone to hold them accountable.

The Sales Cycle: Another way to look at real estate sales activities is to show them as a "sales cycle." Smart, will-be successful new agents jump-start the sales cycle by going right out, talking to lots of people and asking for business.

 BIG IDEAS The business starts when you begin talking to people (see Fig. 3.4).

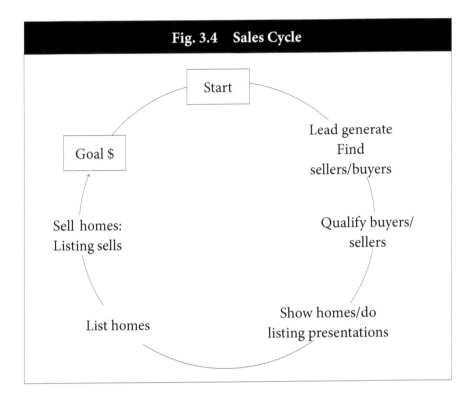

Fig. 3.4   Sales Cycle

From top agent Brian Leavitt: "I have found that you do not even have to do lead generating well. You just have to do it."

Scheduling Your Time so You Make Money

Your Turn. Before I show you specific time commitments for this success formula, write your own weekly schedule here.

After you have made your schedule, evaluate and compare it with the time commitments in figure 3.6.

Fig. 3.5   Your Weekly Schedule

Weekly Schedule

Use one per week. At the end of the week, analyze your results.

NAME:

Suggested Hours Weekly: **What You Did:**

Lead Generating	10	hours
Qualifying buyers/sellers	5	hours
Show properties/listing properties	5	hours
Purchase/sales agreement	5	hours

How could you improve your schedule?

Evaluate Your
Weekly Schedule
Rate yourself in the effectiveness of your weekly schedule:

1-10 (10 is high)

The Schedule for the Successful New Agent

Figure 3.6 shows the time commitments needed to assure a successful start in your career—a start that establishes the habits of a superstar. When you see the total time commitments you need to succeed, you'll see why being a part-time agent will not produce the kind of success most new agents want.

Fig. 3.6 Time Commitments: How to Allocate Your Time as a New Agent to Ensure Quick Success			
Activity	**Daily**	**No./Week**	**Hours**
Lead Generation (Prospecting)	4 Hours	5 Days	20
Open Houses		Once a week	3-4
Floor Time*		1 Day	3
Business Meetings		Once a week	1
Office Education	1 Hour	1 Day	1
Manager/Agent Counseling	1 Hour	Once a week	½
Previewing**	2 Hours	5 Days	10

*Take one segment of floor time, if available in your office; do not count on floor time to deliver the "leads" you'll want to reach your goals.

Here is an example of how to create a schedule from these timeframes. This agent wants to achieve 20 transactions in his first year. {I'm using a 'he' pronoun just as an example. Real estate success is not determined by your age, gender, or background. It's almost solely determined by the work you do.}

Lead generation: All his proactive lead generation (*going out to find people*) is done in the morning, except for Monday, since he has coaching, a meeting, and a tour. He will be lead generating four hours per day, five days a week until he has attained a regular schedule of at least two

Fig. 3.7   Prototype Schedule for the Future Successful Agent

Monday:

> 8:00-8:30 Coaching meeting with manager
> 8:30-9:30 Office meeting
> 9:30-11:00 Office inventory tour
> 11:00-12:00 Lead generate
> 12:00-1:00 Lunch
> 1:00-5:00 Floor time/paperwork (reactive lead generation)

Tuesday:

> Day off, take it!

Wednesday:

> 8:00-12:00 Lead generation (proactive)
> 12:00-1:00 Lunch
> 1:00-4:00 Buyer tour (one of two this week)
> 4:00-5:00 Paperwork

Thursday:

> 8:00-12:00 Lead generation (proactive)
> 12:00-1:00 Lunch
> 1:00-3:00 Previewing
> 3:00-5:00 Paperwork
> 7:00-9:00 Listing presentation

Friday:

> 8:00-12:00 Lead generation (proactive)
> 12:00-1:00 Lunch
> 1:00-4:00 buyer tour (second this week)
> 4:00-5:00 Paperwork

Saturday:

> Day off, take it!

Sunday:

> 11:00-12:00 Paperwork
> 12:00-1:00 Lunch
> 1:00-2:00 Circle prospect around open house (lead generation)
> 2:00-5:00 Open house

Note: Work for scheduling lead generation in the morning. Work toward scheduling two buyer tours/week and one listing presentation per week to sell one home per month and list one home per month.

buyer tours per week and one listing presentation per week to meet his goal of 20 transactions his first year. After attaining a regular schedule of two buyer tours and one listing presentation a week, he will adjust his proactive lead generation schedule to 2 hours per day, 5 days per week.

He also schedules one open house, which is another reactive lead generating activity. In addition, he follows up on Internet leads. Both are "sit and wait for prospects" activities.

Listing presentations and buyer tours: To sell one home a month, he will need to schedule at least two buyer tours per week. To list one home a month, he willl need to schedule one listing presentation per week.

Four Truths About Lead Generation You May Not Be Told

Here's another "10" on the honesty scale: In my opinion, new agents have more incorrect perceptions about lead generating than any other aspect of our business. Why don't you get the real scoop in the interview? Perhaps, like Margie's interviewer, she had no expectations. Or, maybe the interviewer is afraid, if you hear the truth, you'll go somewhere else. Unfortunately, some interviewers lob lots of softball answers to candidates to convince them to join. Later, these agents learn the rest of the story.

Here are the four truths about lead generation:

1. Proactive (go out and meet) lead generation makes agents successful—not reactive (sit and wait).

2. Prioritized lead generating (best sources first) makes agents exceptionally successful—and saves them marketing dollars.

3. In-person and on-phone lead generation is critical to getting leads quickly. Use technology to support, not replace.

4. Setting specific time aside for lead generation assures it gets done.

Let's take them one at a time.

Lead generate in the morning when you're fresh and enthusiastic.

Two Types of Lead Generation: Proactive and Reactive (Active and Passive)

Proactive: You actively contact potential prospects. For instance, if I want to have a party, I call people to come to the party. I don't wait for my friends to use mental telepathy to glean I am having a party. If I did, no one would show up! I must go out and find partygoers and invite them.

From top agent Brian Leavitt: "The most important aspect of proactive lead generation is that I control the outcome. I know the number of people I need to contact __ number of leads."

Reactive: The majority of agents believe somehow potential clients will find them, perhaps through calls to the office, or through open houses. Those two methods of lead generating are termed "reactive" because the agent merely sits and waits and reacts when the prospect contacts him or her.

Go ahead. Schedule yourself to hold an open house. There's nothing wrong with taking advantage of reactive lead generation. However, relying too much on reactive methods (Internet leads, relocation leads, etc.) puts the agent in a tenuous position, especially as markets turn. In a market where buyers are clamoring for homes, buyers will find an agent to help them, and any agent will do! However, in a market where buyers are hard to find, the agent who has relied on the market to drive the buyers to him or her will have no job security.

Go "warm" in with your contacts as fast as you can. That is, pick up the phone rather than continue to email someone. Establish "warm" rapport as soon as possible.

Being Too Reactive Creates a Peaks and Valleys Business

Here's a common thread in an interview. When I ask, "What are you really good at?" the answer sounds like this. "I'm great at follow-up. I sell the home and then call the mortgage people every day. I hound them. My job is to get all the other people involved in the sale (mortgage, title, escrow) to do their jobs."

Sounds like a dutiful agent, right? Invariably, though, when I ask how many transactions this agent completed, it is three to five. Why? Because this agent was really busy following up. Her job description was, "I sell a few homes a year, and then I drive other professionals involved crazy."

Getting too good at some things assures you create a low-income business. I call it a 'peaks and valleys' income contour. The peaks and valleys agent gets a sale or a listing sold. Then, she stops lead generating and start doing the 'fun' stuff—the stuff she is really good at.

I'm not suggesting you don't follow up. I am suggesting you look at your time allotments, your job description, and your results and ask yourself, "What job description am I creating?" Am I doing the activities that create sales, or am I focused on other activities? Track your time allotments to see if you're creating a peaks and valleys business (Fig. 3.8)

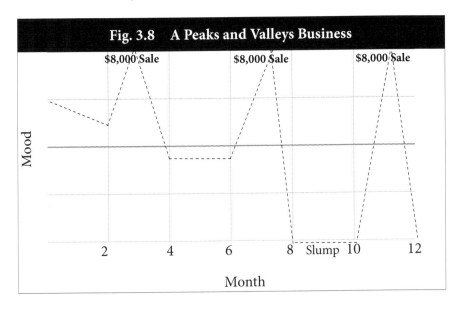

Fig. 3.8   A Peaks and Valleys Business

Worse yet, the reactive agent had not created the success habits of proactive lead generation, because he or she "didn't think I had to."

Prioritize Your Lead Generating Sources

Prioritizing your lead generating sources means that you choose those people you believe will result in the best return for the least money.

In-Person vs. On-Phone? Can I just Use Technology?

Selling real estate isn't a "mail-it-in" or "buy-it-online" business. Yet, many agents are misled into thinking if they only spend lots of money on mail campaigns or technology, the business will come to them without ever having to talk to a human being. Well, maybe, but of course you *pay more* for personal, expert, and knowledgeable service. Remember, this is a people business. Using mail and social media to intersperse with personal contact is fine. However, people buy homes from *people*, not through the mail, and not through computers. Well, sometimes they do, but the commissions are lower, and agents who are order takers don't create referral and long-term businesses. Which type of agent do you want to be?

A Day in the Life of a Successful New Agent

To get even closer to a new agent's real-life daily activity, let's join Marie Smith, a determined, *will-be successful* dedicated agent, as she works through a typically scheduled day. First, a little background about Marie, so you understand the skills she brought to real estate and the challenges facing her as a new agent. Marie was a high school English teacher who became a salesperson, selling hotel convention space. She moved 2,000 miles to the Seattle area just before entering real estate. Even without a background in real estate, she feels good about her sales and writing skills because she developed these skills in her former jobs.

8:00 a.m. Marie goes to the office at this time because she knows she needs to plan activities and do paperwork and research while it is quiet there. She spends one hour in support activities. Because she was in sales, where she had to go out and generate leads, she knows that her career starts there. Her goal is to spend four hours per day, contacting 100 potential leads per week. She knows those time frames and contact numbers will give her the needed number of potential clients and customers to meet her earning expectations of one sale per month as a new agent. Your start-up plan should teach you these numbers and ratios. It should include a spreadsheet for you to keep and analyze.

9:00 a.m. Marie is ready to phone potential buyers and sellers, to ask whether they know someone who wants to buy or sell a home. Marie chose to phone them because she knows few people in the area and realizes that this is a quick method to find prospects. For two hours, Marie talks to 40 homeowners and makes two appointments for that week. This is a normal ratio for Marie. She gets two appointments from 40 calls.

10:00 a.m. Marie takes a break and goes to support activities. To counsel buyers and sellers well, she wants to be sure she knows the available properties on the market. So for 2 hours, Marie previews properties in her area—but not the way low producers preview them. Because she has customers and clients, she looks at properties for a specific purpose. In fact, each support activity that Marie does is related to real customers and clients.

12:00 noon Marie takes a break and has a sandwich at a restaurant near where she lives and works. While there, she hands her card to the waitress and asks for prospects. The waitress refers a friend who wants to buy a property. Marie always takes every opportunity to ask for leads.

1:00 p.m. Marie continues her business-generating activities by knocking on doors in the neighborhood where she lives. A home has been listed there by an agent in her office. With permission from that agent and seller, she tells the neighbors about the new listing and asks for prospects. In order to promote herself, Marie has created a brochure describing the newly listed property including a section about herself. To optimize the effect of these calls, Marie plans to go back into this neighborhood later to tell the neighbors more about this property (an open house, price reduction, listing sold, etc.).

Marie knows that it takes several meetings with people before people will remember her and trust her enough to give her leads, or do business with her themselves. She's establishing herself as an expert in her own neighborhood because she knows that people want to buy and sell real estate with someone they know and trust.

In two hours, Marie knocks on 50 doors and finds 20 households at home. Some of these people already know Marie. One is interested in chatting further with her about selling his home within the next three months. Marie makes an appointment to meet with him and his wife later that week.

3:30 p.m. Marie heads back to the office to return phone calls, handle paperwork, and do other support activities, including social media.

5:00 p.m. She finishes and gets ready to go home. As she gets up from her desk, she receives a phone call. An agent has an offer on Marie's listed property and wants to present the offer that evening. Marie calls home to tell her 15-year-old son that she will not be home for dinner. She asks her son to relay that message to her husband. Marie has taught both men to cook, and they've been supportive of Marie's dedication to her new career. As you know, Marie's goal is to sell a home within a month so she can get a check by month three.

Marie started the business cycle by lead generating aggressively. That does not mean she was overly aggressive toward the people she talked to; it just means she aggressively pursued her plan. By the way, this is a true story. I hired Marie and helped her create and complete her business start-up plan. By following this productivity-focused plan, Marie made more than $85,000 her first year in real estate. (That would be about $400,000 at today's commissions.) Marie credits her success to two things:

- She created and implemented a business start-up plan with large contact numbers and
- She applied her sales skills to real estate.

Marie's Business Start-Up Plan: You've read the description of a typical day in the life of Marie Smith, will-be successful agent. Marie built her days' schedule from the business start-up plan she created, using the principles in this book. She knew this start-up plan would lead her to success. Here is how Marie built her plan for her first three months in the business:

- Marie decided on the results she wanted--number of sales and listings sold.
- Marie figured out the number of buyer showings and listing presentations she needed to complete in her first month to reach her goals.
- Because I (as her manager) told her that 100 contacts a week would assure her the number of buyers and sellers she needed to reach her sales goals, Marie scheduled this in her contact management (twenty calls per day, five days per week).

Fig. 3.9 shows Marie's business start-up plan, expressed as her sales path to success. It is simply a numbers game. Keep your statistics on

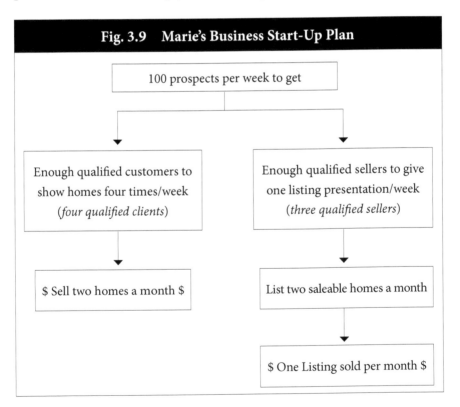

Fig. 3.9   Marie's Business Start-Up Plan

100 prospects per week to get

Enough qualified customers to show homes four times/week *(four qualified clients)*

Enough qualified sellers to give one listing presentation/week *(three qualified sellers)*

$ Sell two homes a month $

List two saleable homes a month

$ One Listing sold per month $

the ratios of activities to results, so you can make adjustments to your plan later on.

Can I Have a Life?

One of a new agent's fears is that he or she will not have a life outside real estate. That need not be the case. You don't have to be available all the time. If you have enough good, qualified clients, you can refer out the leads you can't handle, or don't want to handle. You can even take the day off and refer the client to someone else.

Key to Planning Your Time to Include Days Off: When you are generating a lot of qualified clients and are on your way to fulfilling your income expectations, you muster the intestinal fortitude to turn down potential business or refer it to someone else. Doctors take days off. Accountants take days off. When agents create a good business start-up plan, and consistently work the plan, they create a professional's business. They earn their days off.

Still, don't let me kid you. For the first year in the business, you will work more crazy hours, more total hours, and more consecutive days than you ever imagined. Why? Because you want to succeed. You love the challenge of completing the sales cycle of selling homes and listing homes that sell. You love making people happy with exceptional service, and you're motivated by their expressions of appreciation.

Weekends and Evenings: As a new agent, establishing your own independent business, you are truly an entrepreneur. If you were opening your first restaurant on a prayer and a shoestring, you would do everything possible to ensure success. You would be there early in the morning and late at night, doing any job that had to be done. It is the same with your real estate career. So, you work weekends to hold open houses, prospect, and show homes. On weekends, more buyers are available, and both sellers are generally available for listing presentations.

For a new agent, not being able to work weekends, or refusing to do so, is like opening your restaurant from 10 a.m. to noon. It may be convenient for you, but it surely isn't convenient for your diners—and they pay your bills.

For New Agents, Is There Life Outside Real Estate? There had better be; otherwise, new agents suffer burnout, the emotional overload from expending a lot of energy with the goal buried in what becomes grinding daily activity. To have a life outside real estate, new agents must establish an effective business start-up plan. In that schedule, agents must include at least one day off per week. Every six to eight weeks, all agents should schedule three to four days away.

Time Management—The Key to Retaining Your Sanity: For most agents, real estate sales are a completely new and different world, a world we throw ourselves into, immersing in the curious language, exciting sales cycle, and dismaying, depressing reality of rejection. For many, this immersion also causes us to bury the real self, sometimes to the point of forgetting that we are valuable, knowledgeable, capable people. We all need to continue taking part in activities that give us a sense of ourselves, that remind us of our unique, intrinsic value, and share in life beyond real estate.

For me, that meant continuing to play music gigs, even though it resulted in getting about four hours of sleep on the weekends. Holding weekend public open houses at that time was a constant battle against sleep, a battle that I lost a couple of times! However, doing two disparate things at once was important to my self-esteem. It helped maintain a balance between something I knew well and something that was completely strange, new, and challenging.

Maintain Confidence and Sense of Yourself

Schedule leisure time to pursue a hobby, activity, pleasure, visits with friends, walks, or get out of town—whatever you do to enjoy the *real you*. Be willing to give up some potential income to maintain a sense of balance in your life. You'll need it when things get rough. In addition, create methods to manage your attitude—to stay "up" during those first challenging months.

"I'm Available 24 Hours a Day": I see that on agents' business cards. I listen to their voicemail: "I will return your call within fifteen minutes." Be careful not to set up expectations you may not be able to meet.

 Take your home phone number off those business cards. Do you want them calling you at 10 p.m. to ask you to explain points?

Control your time by controlling your communication devices. Give people times when you will return their calls. Tell them when you will be available—and when you aren't. Explain how you work. In other words, train them in how to communicate with you.

Gaining the Support and Cooperation of Your Family

This focus on real estate can be disruptive to the rhythm of your family life. In addition to scheduling days off and time to be *you*, it is important to discuss the nature of your new job with your family. Here are several important steps to take with your spouse, family or other household members:

- Ask your family to read sections of this book and discuss the nature of this entrepreneurial job.

- Discuss a new schedule for home chores with your family so different family members prepare meals and otherwise cover tasks you usually perform. You may not be able to do the same chores to the same level of excellence that you did while you were living your prior life.

- Build some rewards for members of your family to be given when you reach your goals. Ask yourself, "What's in it for them?" Ask them the same question. Sit down with your family, decide on rewards and how those rewards are tied to reaching your goals. Create some mutual goals so that your career becomes part of your family's long-term goals.

- Explain the nature of this job to your family, what you will do to make money, your time frames for activities and goals, and the potential scheduling conflicts that could cut into your family time. Ask each member of your family if they understand your new commitments, and if they are willing to support your efforts.

- Show your spouse/partner your office and introduce your spouse/ partner and manager. Many times, agents leave real estate sales quickly because the spouse doesn't understand the nature of the job, or the spouse isn't willing to support the activities and erratic time schedule of the new agent. It's important for your spouse to see where and with whom you're going to work, and get a chance to get to know your manager. That way, all the parties can empathize with the stresses and time commitments that the new agent will have to manage.

(One of my reviewers, a newer agent, added "That's an understatement!")

> The Good News: *That first paycheck really enhances the partner/ spouse's view of your career!*

How to Plan for After the "Newbie" Phase

To be successful, you will keep generating leads actively throughout your career. In that sense, you always follow the business start-up plan. An evolutionary process occurs, though, as you spend more time in the business. As a new agent, if you make 100 contacts per week for your first month, you'll find you've generated *so* much business that you'll have to cut back on your volume of contacts. But *do not stop contacting!* Think of lead generating like riding a bicycle. When you stop pedaling, you fall over. By measuring the number of contacts you make, and the results you get, you'll find a happy medium, enabling you to generate the leads and income you want and still have a life.

Find someone who will coach you using your business start-up plan as your "game plan."

I don't mean someone who will just answer your questions, or "mentor" you. I mean someone who holds you accountable to those business start-up plan goals you said you wanted to achieve.

Another Method of Gaining Support: A Mentor or Coach

Mark, a new agent, went through the same patterns many new agents endure. He sat around for his first two months, confused about what to do. He found it fascinating and comforting to preview properties, learn new technology, and organize his files. As time went by, though, he got frantic because his money was running out, and he had no sales.

When I became the manager of that office, I immediately found him a peer coach—a seasoned agent who would jump-start him every day to go out and lead generate. I gave the coach and Mark the start-up plan I've shown you and told them that's what they were to use.

For the first week, his peer coach met with Mark daily. I met with Mark every three to seven days for the first month. Armed with that level of guidance and support, within a month Mark had his first sale. In four months, he had two sales and four listings. We taught Mark how to analyze his business numbers and manage his career to higher levels. Now he does it on his own.

By reminding you of what you want, the coach helps you stay focused, the biggest problem for "people" people! Your coach will coach you in those business-producing activities you've identified as critical to your goals—those activities from a proven business start-up plan. Who could this coach be? Your manager, or an agent in your office who's building his business, while still more experienced than you.

Business Sources Evolve with Your Business

Experienced agents who maintain successful careers still lead generate for potential clients, but they may evolve to different sources. The best source of an experienced agent's business is people who have previously bought and sold homes through him or her.

Past Client and Referral Business Is the Name of the Game: According to a recent Realtor® survey, only about one-third of an agent's business was generated from former clients and referrals. This doesn't mean agents can sit back and wait for the phone to ring. As long as the experienced agent keeps in touch with these people and asks for leads, he or she can maintain a good income. Very successful agents attribute more than 75% of their income from referrals. That's the kind of business to create.

Summary

As a typical day in the life of a will-be successful new real estate agent was described, how did you feel? Were you excited and challenged by the fact that you could complete activities each day that ensured a check? Did you find yourself trying to reject those activities in favor of research and support activities? Were you anxious about diving right into the business?

Did you feel confident that you could devote that much energy and time to success? Or did you feel that you just didn't want to work that much? What were your family considerations? What challenges might you have there? Overall, how does this practical, everyday picture of a will-be successful agent differ from your earlier perceptions?

Big Ideas from Chapter 3

- A will-be successful agent's daily business start-up plan revolves around a half-day of business-generating activities.
- Putting in 20 hours a week assures a low-producing business.
- If the interviewer does not provide a job description or expectations in the interview, it probably means you'll get no guidance to start your business.

- Waiting for business to come to you assures a low-paying career.

- People buy homes from people, not technology.

- As a real estate salesperson, you are truly an entrepreneur, in charge of your own schedule and time management.

 ## *Get a Jump-Start on Success*

- Make your own schedule. Compare it to the timeframes for success (figure 3.5).

- Use a prioritized business start-up plan. Don't guess and make your own. Compare it to the prototypes here, along with time frames and expectations.

- If you are ready to launch your career, have the conversations with your spouse/partner to get their full understanding and cooperation.

CHAPTER 4

How Much Money Can You Make?

"I came into real estate thinking that, with my sales background, I'd make six figures my first year. I had friends in the business, and I just knew I could be as successful as they were! After a few months, I found it was more challenging than I'd imagined. It took me longer to 'learn the ropes' than I thought it would. But I love it! Although I didn't quite break six figures my first year, I laid the groundwork for my second year. It's exciting, challenging, hard work."

~Kay Zatine, top sales in her first year, formerly a radio salesperson

In This Chapter

- Incomes: What Is Really "Average"?
- What Mega-Agents Make
- Four Categories of Earners
- The Part-Time Option
- More Career Choices
- Big Ideas
- Get a Jump-Start on Your Business

One of the most common questions would-be agents ask is, "How much money can I make?" In this chapter, you will see fact vs. fiction. Here is another "10" on the honesty scale. You may be told in the interview that agents make $400,000 a year. Some do, because they have built their businesses over a period of years—and they work hard, but very few make $400,000 their *first* year! I'm not trying to be discouraging, just realistic. Here are the statistics and some expectations for your first year and beyond.

Incomes: What's Really "Average"?

What does the average real estate agent make? The best figures available come from the National Association of REALTORS®, (NAR), which surveys its members regularly. Even though this is not a survey of all licensees (about one-half of all licensees are REALTORS®), NAR consists of the "cream of the crop"—those licensees who are willing to pay dues to contribute to the professionalism of their industry. NAR members tend to treat real estate as a career, not an avocation. The latest NAR figures tell us the median gross income for a Realtor® is $43,300.

Note: That's gross income, *before* expenses. Is that less than you thought or have been told? Maybe. But that includes all those who have just started in the business, those who aren't very committed, and those who just want to do a couple of deals a year.

What Difference a Few Years Make

Many people think real estate sales is an easy way to make lots of money. True, it is a great way to be in business for yourself without a large capital outlay, and it can be a wonderful career. But, like any other entrepreneurial endeavor, it requires dedication, tenacity, and determination. Most importantly, your success is really up to you, not your manager, not your company, and not your fellow agents.

What Newer Realtor® Salespeople Make: According to NAR, agents with less than two years in the business have median gross incomes of $8500. Agents with more than sixteen years in the business have median gross incomes of $75,000. Twenty-six percent made more than $150,000. As you can see from the figures, it takes a while for an agent to get established. It takes two to three years to build a "dream career" in real estate. Why? Because, as you meet and help more people, your potential for referrals grows.

An Example of a "Not Average" Start-Up Agent: Nada had just moved to the Seattle area. She had never been in real estate sales but had sold hotel convention space in Cincinnati. She also had writing skills from her background as an English teacher. Nada and I worked together to create a business start-up plan based on the principles in Chapter 3. In fact, my experience with Nada, and other "not average" new agents showed me exactly what that start-up plan needed to be.

Nada was a virtual whirlwind of energy and activity. She proactively lead generated to find many potential buyers. With this work, she found *so* many potential clients that she made a sale her first month. She completed more than 35 transactions her first year. In her fourth year she made $450,000 without an assistant (that would be about $800,000 today). She is an example of talent, enthusiasm, desire, sales skills, and working hard at the right activities.

If You Don't Want to Be "Average": Don't copy what "average" agents do. "Average" agents start with no start-up plan—or a poor one. They just hang out at the office and let things happen. Or, they go to the training program, learn how to fill out forms, and think that sales will just appear. In fact, only about five percent of new agents start with a proven start-up plan. Reasons I've heard are:

- "I didn't know I needed one."
- "I thought my company training would suffice."
- "My manager didn't tell me I needed one."
- "I'm independent. I don't need to have anyone tell me what to do."
- "New agents don't need business plans."

Isn't it naive to believe that anyone could succeed in a new business without a proven business blueprint? Yet, real estate is one of the few industries that has kicked and screamed about structure and systems! (The common comment is, "Real estate is different.") No, it is a business too. And successful businesses create and follow business plans. New agents need business start-up plans—blueprints for success.

Commitment + Time + Exceptional Income

Agents are staying in the business longer. Between 1993 and today, the average number of years a Realtor® has been in business has increased from six to eight.

Look at a real estate career to pay off in three to six years. As my friend and "super-trainer" Bonnie Sparks, says, "You're not *in* the real estate business anymore. You *have* a real estate *business* now." Long-term thinking and business planning, including budgeting, assures your career success. (Budgeting is addressed in a later chapter, so you know your income and expenses).

What the Mega-Agents Make—and How

You have already seen agents who make more money work more hours. You also know they have been in the business more years.

Here's how mega-agents make $250,000 and more:

1. They build a team of assistants, buyers' agents, and listing agents to multiply their time and effectiveness. They hold their team members accountable for results.
2. They are highly skilled salespeople, and have studied, practiced, and mastered sales skills. They teach these skills to their team.
3. They use detailed systems and processes for each part of their business, and expect staff and team members to follow those systems.
4. They have sophisticated communication methods to stay in touch with their previous clients and their "sphere of influence"—those people most likely to work with them and send referrals.

5. They run their businesses with business plans and budgets.

6. They use technology wisely to support their businesses.

7. They either have a staff person who manages their finances, or they hire an accounting firm to manage income and expenses and analyze results.

In a nutshell, successful REALTORS® create businesses that are run like, and are as productive as, many complete real estate offices. In a later chapter, I'll explain more about the "business-within-the-business" concept that's allowing agents to create real businesses that are salable.

You Get Back What You Put Into It

You might ask, "Why would I want to go into business for myself? I'll make *less* than I'm making now as an employee." We know, though, that averages really do not represent real life. For example, the "average" American family consists of 1.5 children. Looking at an average real estate income is misleading. People enter real estate for many reasons, which are reflected in their incomes:

- Some want to make a little extra money— and that is all they will make.

- Some are dedicated and serious about real estate as a career so they set career goals and work hard.

- Some, unfortunately, want someplace to go so they can say they go to work. Guess how much money they make.

Three Major Variables Determine a Person's Income in Real Estate

1. Reasons for entering the field (earn a little extra money or career change).

2. Motivation to succeed in real estate.

3. Kind and *amount of activities* the person is willing to do to succeed in real estate.

Your *internal motivation to succeed* is the *most* important determinant of success. It's much more important than who you know, the area where you work, or your age or background.

Is There a Best Time to Enter Real Estate?

No. For good salespeople, there are no bad markets, unless it's a major, long-term economic catastrophe. Even then, smart agents know how to help people through tough times. You may have heard that there are good times to go into real estate, right? A good time is when rates are low, buyers are buying, and sellers are cooperative. Dream on! Those three situations rarely go together.

No "Perfect" Markets. When lots of new agents enter the market, there's much more competition. In addition, "good markets" (low rates, sunny economic predictions) make buyers and sellers feel *less* need for an agent, or that *any* agent will do. Clients need agents when the going gets tough! That's when good agents really get going.

Doing Better in a "Terrible" Market: When the market is sluggish is a great time to enter real estate. I had been selling for six years, and each year had increased my income. I had attained recognition as one of the top 10 agents at my 400-agent company, after having been in real estate about four years. Then the interest rates ballooned to 20 percent. Many agents got out of the business while I continued to make more money.

Visiting another office, I ran into one of their top agents. Bob was consistently among the top one percent of all agents in the U. S. We started talking about the high interest rates. I told him, although I was doing better than ever, I was concerned. I heard this was a tough market, and "you can't make money in real estate when interest rates are high."

Bob, "Mr. Real Estate Success," assured me that good agents do better in slow markets, and that I would continue to do better. Why? Good agents *work the market they're given*, while poor agents sit around and complain about the market.

When homes aren't selling because of high interest rates, good agents help sellers create new marketing strategies to attract serious buyers:

creative financing, better pricing, and better staging of the home to show. Good agents find buyers who want to buy, and help them structure the transaction so it's a "win-win" for everyone.

From the statistics I've provided, you can see why coming in and out of real estate sales doesn't give you the time, experience, or backlog of happy clients you need to build a superstar career.

How the Area Where You Work Affects Your Income

The higher the home prices, the greater the sales commission. So, in market areas where there is a large, expensive inventory of homes, agents think it is easier to make money than in a smaller, less expensive market area. However, two things are wrong with that thinking:

There is much more competition in high-end markets. Bellevue, a suburb of Seattle, Washington, is an example of an area where the home prices are high. It is a transferee destination, and the agents are highly professional and competitive. Generally, experienced sellers, selling their expensive homes, ask their friends and business connections for recommendations, and choose an agent who has been referred to them by several sources. This is typically an agent who has built a stellar reputation through the years. It isn't realistic to expect to waltz in and take away the high- end referral business that those agents have cultivated for 20 years!

Agents build larger, more effective businesses through referrals. The more homes you sell, the more referrals you get (if you do a great job and keep in touch, asking for referrals).

Sell More Homes. To create steadily growing businesses, agents should concentrate on selling *more* homes, not just making big commissions from one home. More 'revenue units' means more happy people. More happy people mean more referrals for you, now and forever.

More Revenue Units and Smaller and/or Less Expensive Market. The beauty of a smaller market is that you can build your career on the best source of long-term business—referrals. You will have less competition, and your cost of living is lower. I have watched highly professional agents in these smaller communities simply overcome their competition by working their businesses as I described in the "mega-agent" business in this chapter.

Four Categories of Earners

Some people want to go into real estate, not to give it their best effort, but to make a few easy bucks. However, the bucks *aren't* easy, but they *are* few!

Categorized by their expectations, salespeople fall into four groups. My surveys show that there are average income ranges for each of these groups (see fig. 4.1):

1. **Part-Timers:** These agents want to make a little money in their spare time, or in retirement, or working weekends, etc. As you might imagine, the average income for this group is a few hundred to a few thousand dollars per year. The disturbing fact about this group is that they can create poor customer satisfaction because they are not dedicated to building a career through superior customer service. Since they have other interests, they do not have follow-up systems, processes, or supports that make customers feel as though they got superior service. They are notorious for not returning phone calls, emails, and texts. If the client isn't a quick 'slam dunk', some of them just won't stay engaged with that client.

   If you are a part-timer, or know one, do not take these comments personally. These are generalizations I have gleaned through observing thousands of part-timers. I do know a part-timer who is a wonderful achiever. He is a schoolteacher who works real estate in the summers, evenings, and weekends. He has established a solid career over two decades of steady work. (Please note I could only point to one....)

2. **Underachievers:** These agents fail to produce much income because they do not find enough qualified prospects fast enough to list and sell a reasonable number of homes each year. They

may spend time at the office collating, organizing, learning technology, and attending meetings. They love the social aspect of real estate—getting together with their agent friends for wine, etc., but they do not complete many business-producing activities. Generally, they know what to do, but do not do these activities consistently.

The average for this group is about $7,000 to $25,000 per year. They get some business by waiting for prospects to come to them (an iffy way to guarantee your income).

3. **Business Maintainer:** These agents have all the money they need, and still sell real estate because they enjoy the work. They make enough yearly to meet their needs (around $25,000 to $50,000+). Many times, business maintainers have another source of income. Their strategy is to wait for business, so they expend relatively little effort actively lead generating for buyers and sellers.

4. **Careerists:** These agents look at real estate as a business career. They are willing to do the sales-generating activities in the numbers required to start and perpetuate a successful real estate business. They are willing to build their careers steadily through the years.

The income range for careerists in their second to third year is $50,000 to $100,000+ (Figs. 4.1 and 4.2). I have personally hired and trained people who, in their first, second and third years, made $60,000 to $400,000+. The long-term earning potential (from approximately year three onward) for the dedicated careerist is $100,000 to $500,000+.

 Beware the 'professional': He's always in the office, working. He is organized. He knows all the answers.

Before you ask advice, find the people who are successful careerists, not just fonts of knowledge.

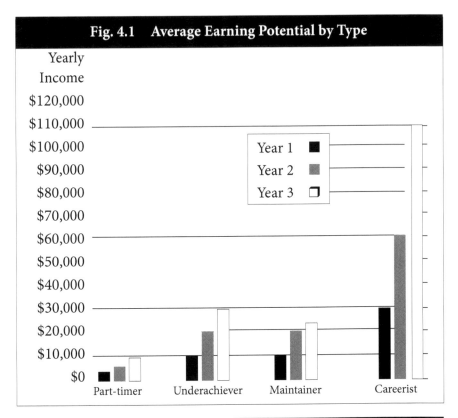

Fig. 4.1   **Average Earning Potential by Type**

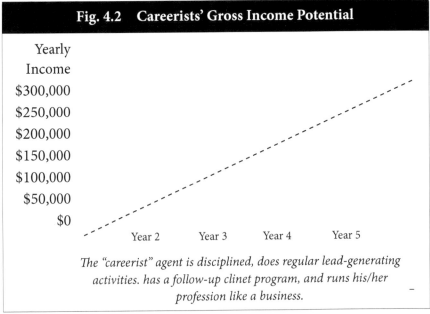

Fig. 4.2   **Careerists' Gross Income Potential**

The "careerist" agent is disciplined, does regular lead-generating activities. has a follow-up clinet program, and runs his/her profession like a business.

What is a "Professional"? It is important to differentiate the term *careerist* from the term *professional*. In the real estate industry, a professional is known as a real estate agent who:

- Has been working at least a few years in real estate sales
- Has attained more knowledge about real estate than he or she had as a new agent
- Works reasonably long hours (sometimes)

What's left out of this definition? Income. Using the definition mentioned, experienced real estate salespeople call themselves professionals even if they made $1.95 from real estate the year before.

That's why I didn't use the word "professional" to define a successful real estate agent.

To me, a successful real estate agent makes an income commensurate with other professions.

The Part-Time Option

The National Association of REALTORS® defines a "part-timer" as a Realtor® working fewer than twenty hours in a week. My observation is that the gap between full-time and part-time salespeople keeps widening. Why? Working in real estate sales part-time is becoming more difficult for the following reasons:

- The start-up costs of real estate sales are higher than ever.
- Licensing requirements, including pre-license and post-license education, are escalating and will continue to escalate.
- As more careerists enter the field, they aggressively seek out business, leaving less of the business to fall into the part-timer's lap. (It's more difficult for the part-timer to "pick off" the sales of unsuspecting buyers who just stumble into any home and buy it.")

- Agents must invest more money and time and get more education to stay in the business. They must invest in technology to compete with serious careerists.
- The public is demanding better quality service. They interview several agents before they begin to look for a home. They invite several agents to compete for the listing. They demand résumés and testimonials. They are being advised to choose their agent carefully, just as they would choose their doctor.

The Costs of Failure are High for All. For twelve years, I taught courses for the Real Estate Brokerage Managers Council, an affiliate of the National Association of REALTORS®. These courses lead to the CRB (Certified Real Estate Broker) designation. I asked hundreds of managers and owners across the nation to estimate how much it costs to hire an agent who does not make it. The average six-month costs for companies range from $10,000 to $30,000.

> Trend: *Agent hiring costs continue to go up, with companies' technology, hardware, software, and training costs escalating.*

You can see why good companies are careful whom they hire. With that large of an investment, you would be careful too. In addition, companies want to keep providing a higher level of customer service through hiring and training dedicated, service-oriented careerists. What is the cost of failure to an agent? Money invested and time wasted. Worst of all, self-esteem goes in the dumper!

The Real-Life Challenges for a Part-Timer

Here are some of the sales situations part-timers can find themselves in:

- You have another job, and a buyer you have been working with wants to purchase a property now. The buyer knows there has been a lot of interest in the property, and is afraid, if he doesn't get his offer to purchase signed in the next two hours, he might lose the deal. How will you explain that you cannot help him now because you have to go to your other job? Could you miss earning a commission when the buyer, in frustration, goes to another agent? Will you gain referrals from this client?

- An offer to purchase comes in on your listing, and the seller expects you to represent him as he looks at the offer. However, it is time to go to your other job. How do you explain that you cannot represent the seller's best interests, especially when he is paying thousands of dollars for representation? What is your level of customer service? Is it high enough to justify the commission you charge? Will you gain referrals from this client?

- How will you generate prospects fast enough to earn income in your first few months while your expenses continue? As you saw in the weekly schedule for a new agent (Fig. 3.5), careerists who want to replace their previous income fast, and build a successful career, plan to spend four hours a day finding prospects.

My observations: Sometimes, part-timers register for my training/ start-up business program, *Up and Running in Real Estate*. Although they have the best of intentions, they just don't have the time to build a reliable business (build a database; follow up with potential clients; design marketing programs; create presentations, etc.). In addition, they have responsibilities in their present job that keep pulling them back to that job. From my hiring and training hundreds of new salespeople, I've also drawn these conclusions. It takes an exceptional person, willing to work 12-16 hours a day, to build that real estate business to the point they can rely on it and leave her other job.

How About Part-Time Until You Hit It Big Enough to Quit That Second Job?

You will need at least three-months' savings, and better yet, six months', since your commission checks won't be coming in from day one (more later in another chapter). Frequently, a person who does not have sufficient savings to cover the first few months considers keeping the old job while starting in real estate part-time. The agent thinks it possible to earn enough in real estate part-time to pay expenses and launch a career. However, it takes a great deal of effort, time, dedication, and skill just to start generating prospects. Therefore, the person trying to hold an old job while starting a new sales career quickly becomes discouraged.

Alternatives. Instead of attempting to start a new sales career while holding down another job, here are some alternatives:

- Borrow sufficient capital from some source to go into real estate full-time from the beginning. You will need a few months to get your business started and those few months require intensive, 100% effort.

- One of the most successful agents in our area told me he borrowed on each of his charge cards so he could go into the business. Was he ever compelled to succeed! I'm not suggesting you put your credit at risk. I am suggesting that you take actions that demonstrate your dedication to succeed.

- Work in a real estate company, or as an agent's assistant in a staff position, to learn the business from that perspective. Then go full-time into sales. One of my office secretaries, at age 23, did just that. She can be much more organized, understand all the jargon and, from watching agents operate, know whom to emulate and what contributes to providing high levels of customer satisfaction.

As we discussed in the chapter on behavior profiles, people who are wonderful at staff jobs may not like sales. They are not comfortable lead generating. You've learned the truism: If you don't lead generate, you don't get paid!" Before you decide to sell homes, "shadow" a successful salesperson for a few days to find out exactly what that salesperson does to generate income—with people and outside the office. Take a behavioral profile and have it interpreted by someone who understands profiles and their natural "fit" with certain jobs.

- Work at two salaried jobs to save sufficient capital to go into real estate. You will find that better than entering real estate part-time. (One of the traits of successful agents is that they have frequently worked at two jobs to attain their goals.)

If you must start your career as a part-timer, give yourself a deadline to become full-time. Ask your broker to help you enforce that deadline.

Otherwise, in my experience, you will try to continue both jobs, and ultimately abandon your real estate goals.

More Career Choices: Coaches, Teams, Assistants and More

Besides deciding whether to become a full- or part-time agent, you have other career choices:

- Hire an accountability coach (the manager or a professional coach affiliated with that office)
- Find a coach or a peer coach
- Become a team member
- Become an assistant

Which of these may be good choices for you?

Find a coach or a peer coach: I hope your manager will become your accountability coach. As you interview, you'll find managers promise to "coach you." However, that quickly becomes a "got a minute" answerman function instead of focused, linear, goal-oriented action coaching. You do not need a coach just for answers. You need a coach to hold you accountable to your goals and the action plan you and your coach create.

Choosing a Coach: Here are three important points to consider as you search for a coach:

- The specific program should be highly organized and precisely outlined with checklists and systems. Ask, "What system are you going to use to coach me?" You need a specific game plan because you are new. You have no history.

- The specific program should be related to a "game plan"—a business start-up plan. Ask, "What business start-up plan are you going to use?"(See it, don't just hear about it".

- A coach should be trained and coached themselves. Ask, "What is your coaching background, and what sales principles do you believe in?" "Do you, or have you had a business coach?"

Watch out for: Your coach is trained and dedicated to your success and is following a proven game plan (otherwise you'll be paying just to talk to someone every once in a while).

Positives: *Having a coach keeps you on track, motivated, and, ideally, inspired to reach your goals.*

Types of Coaches

Professional Coach: Someone trained to coach, who uses a specific program and who is *paid* to be your coach. If you are considering a professional coach, find out the specific program the coach will use. Get expectations in writing. Give the coach your expectations in writing. You should expect to sign a three- to twelve-month contract.

Manager Coach or In-Office Coach: Someone who may be *trained* as a coach, who has agreed to coach you. May be paid from your commissions or from a combination of office/your commissions. May be paid hourly by the agent. Be sure this coach is prepared to be your accountability coach, has a specific schedule with you, and a specific start-up plan to coach you. Otherwise, you are just getting an "advice session."

Whether you affiliate with a professional or in-office coach, you should expect to:

- Be held accountable to prioritized activities
- Have a proven, prioritized business start-up system to which you are coached
- Avoid regarding your coach as 'answer man'
- Be terminated if you do not take action steps as agreed

Peer Coach: Someone in the office, an agent, who has agreed to be your coach. However, this arrangement could include such activities are:

- Answers questions
- Lets you "shadow them" (see how they do a listing/buyer presentation or offer presentation)
- Holds you accountable to your goals or refers you to a 'higher authority' if there's no activity or results

Many peer coaches do not have a coaching program to coach to and haven't been trained. They are also at a loss with what to do if the agent refuses to do the work.

Unmatched Expectations. In my experience, the new agent has the high hopes that the peer coach will fulfill his dreams of whatever coaching is to him. Frequently, the new agent thinks all she needs is someone always there to answer questions. The peer coach is hoping the agent just does not ask too many questions!

If you are going to work with a peer coach, get in writing exactly what that peer coach is willing to do with and for you. Get in writing what you are expected to do with and for your peer coach. Bad peer coaching can turn into a nightmare for both parties.

Agents' Advice: Dozens of experienced agents have told me they wish they had started with a professional coach. If you can find one to trust and to follow, you will shorten your learning curve dramatically and easily pay for the coaching fee. Plus, you will establish a successful long-term career.

Getting a Mentor

What is a "mentor"? There is not a clearly defined job function for "mentor". Mentors are usually seasoned agents who offer to help new agents. They may:

- Offer advice
- Allow you to shadow them
- Ask you to do parts of their business

New agents love the thought of a mentor because they have so many questions. They think the mentor will be their "answer man." I have observed that having an "answer man" (or woman) does not guarantee success. In fact, it may impede an agent getting into action. How? An agent may think he needs more and more information before he will act. Then, he just keeps coming to the mentor for every question under the sun. The more the new agent knows, the more frightened he becomes. Plus, the advice received from the mentor may not be in the new agent's best interest.

Get expectations from both parties in writing.

 BIG IDEAS Why is the mentor willing to help you? What's in it for the mentor? What does the mentor expect from you? How much will you pay?

Joining a Team

As you interview, you may be invited to join an office team. That means you will be essentially working for a "rainmaker," a lead agent who generates leads for those on his team. Of course, those leads cost money, and the rainmaker takes about half the income from the team member for lead generation and other services, like administrative support.

Teaming helps agents obtain leads as they start up. While agents earn the most in commissions when they generate their own leads, a new agent may feel more secure paying someone else for leads. There is a downside to this approach. Agents can become complacent and sit and *wait* for leads, since they believe their rainmaker should supply all their leads. They will not lead generate—until they get tired of paying someone else.

> Positives: *You may be able to jump-start your career with leads given to you.*

Watch out for: Be careful to choose a rainmaker who really has enough good leads to distribute to you. Sit in on her team meeting to see how she manages the team. Find out if and how the rainmaker will train you.

- Ask how much turnover there has been on the team.
- Ask whether you can sell and list houses outside the team—and how much the rainmaker will charge you if you do.
- See the specific systems the rainmaker will use with his team. Lack of systems means the team will not operate as a team, and you will be left trying to figure out how to take action on your own.
- Read the contract the rainmaker asks you to sign. Be sure you understand the consequences of your involvement. Evaluate how good a leader that rainmaker is.

Some rainmakers are great salespeople, but lousy leaders. As a result, their team never jells. Most team leaders ultimately expect their team members to generate their own leads in addition to team leads. If you cannot meet the rainmaker's expectations, you are terminated. Be willing and ready to take the responsibilities of team membership seriously.

Starting Over: When you leave the team, you are generally starting again as a new agent, since you have not generated your own leads.

Become an Assistant

> **BIG IDEAS** Assistants see a different side of the business. They see what the agent isn't doing well (like paperwork and follow-up). What they don't see is the people-interaction — which the agent does exceedingly well. So, assistants think that the business is a task/technical one. That's the wrong emphasis.

Some agents have the bright idea (they think) to become an assistant to "learn the business." I have seen a few assistants become good agents. Here is the rub. Remember the information about behavioral profiles? The assistant profile is *task*-oriented, while the salesperson profile is *people*-oriented. So, while the assistant criticizes the agent for not doing paperwork, the agent is out in the field selling houses. (Paperwork is the assistant's job.) The agent's and assistant's skills are supposed to *complement* each other, not *duplicate* each other.

If you become an assistant, you will learn the paperwork and process side of the business. If you have the right profile and background, you may become very good at it, but the more you love being an assistant, the more you will hate selling real estate!

Summary

At the beginning of this chapter, we posed a question about earning potential. As you can see, there is not one simple answer. Here are the major points concerning income expectations:

- Although the median income for real estate salespeople is modest, that median represents agents whose business goals differ.

- The dedicated careerist can earn an income comparable to that of other professions, an income that grows as the careerist competence and sales record grow over a period of years.

- Social, cultural, and economic trends make it increasingly difficult for a salesperson to enter part-time or to earn income that exceeds expenses.

- Real estate incomes are mainly determined by a person's motivation for entering real estate, his or her income needs.

Big Ideas from Chapter 4

- Although the median income for real estate salespeople is modest, that median represents agents whose business goals differ from one another—and certainly may differ from yours.

- It takes over one year to establish a budding career. (It is not a 3-month trial business.)

- Most agents increase their incomes significantly from years three to ten.

- You HAVE a business; you are not just in the business.

- Your tenacity and motivation to succeed are the most important determinants of your success.

- Work the market you're given; don't wait for the market to become what you want.

- Making buyers and sellers happy is key to establishing a long- term business. In other words, more "happy revenue units" (people) is better.

- Do not be lured to focus only on highest priced homes for prestige value. Selling three million-dollar homes per year will not create a long-term business! Establish transactions by making as many people as you can happy; then move up the price ladder.

- Decide what type of career you want and join the office where you think that goal will be supported.

- Weigh the pros and cons of your career choices before you jump to any conclusions.

 ## *Get a Jump-Start on Success*

Ask yourself which kind of agent do you want to be?

- Interview five agents. Ask for their daily schedules. Compare their schedules to Nada's. Take a guess: How much money do you think each of these five agents makes? It will directly correspond to the number of times agents lead generate, qualify buyers, show homes, do listing presentations, list homes that sell, and represent sellers at offers.

- Before you decide to be a part-timer, talk to ten part-time agents. Find out how they are doing, how much time they devote to the business, and what their challenges are. What do you think motivates them to grow their businesses? Consider some of the alternatives to part-time explained in this chapter.

- If you are considering becoming a team member, speak to present and past team members of that particular team and ask the questions from this chapter.

CHAPTER 5

What It Costs and When
You'll Break Even

"You may fall short of your goal but reach high. Open yourself to all possibilities. Business is everywhere. Are you getting better? If you are going in the right direction slowly it will get you there faster than going in the wrong direction and starting over. So, adopt good plans and habits."

~ Connie Kruse

In This Chapter

- What It Costs to Get Started
- The Tools of the Trade You'll Need—Including Your Car
- How to Establish a Personal and Professional Budget: Your expenses for the first six months
- How Long to a Paycheck?
- When You'll Break Even
- How Many Sales Is Enough to Create a Great Business?
- Big Ideas
- Get a Jump-Start to Success

What It Costs to Get Started

Jerry started his real estate career thinking he would receive a paycheck within a month. He had been in printing sales and management for, as he said, "Practically my whole life, so I knew I could sell." However, he did not know how much money was going to go out each month just to get him into business and keep him there.

"I didn't know the time frame to find a client, show homes, sell him something, and wait to get paid."

Jerry's advice: "Before you go into real estate, you need to know your start-up expenses, ongoing expenses, and a time frame (if you work hard) for expecting to earn that first paycheck."

So, with Jerry's advice in mind, this chapter explains an agent's expenses, time frames, and monetary expectations for his first year in the real estate business.

Initial Costs Are Relatively Small

When you enter real estate sales, you are immediately in business for yourself.

Fig. 5.1   Agent Approximate Start-up Costs

Pre-license course:
Pre-license course $300-$500
Test fee $100-$150 (per attempt)

At affiliation:
Licensing fee (2 years) $100-200
Fingerprint fee $40-50
Multiple listing fee $400-500
Lockboxes $10-15 per month for ekey mobile app (+$50 activation)
Realtor® dues $600-800

(In some states, MLS and Realtors® are one entity; in other states, like Washington state, they are separate; dues are prorated by the month you join)

Fig. 5.1   Agent Approximate Start-up Costs (Cont'd)

Company joining fees:
$150-300

Tools of the trade:
$300 (briefcase, supplies, signs, etc. See Fig. 5.3)
Total: $2050+

Recommended:
Laptop $1,000
Contact management software (CRM) $50-$100/month

Pre-license Costs

The initial costs of entry are relatively small. Fig. 5.1 is an itemization of typical initial costs. These are the costs you will incur before and immediately after you are licensed. They include studying for your real estate license, affiliating with a company, activating your license, and beginning your career.

Budgeting: Materials and Services You will Need

Fig. 5.2 is a sample list of the materials and services essential in real estate sales. Refer to this list when you interview. Find out which services are provided and paid for by the company, which are shared by agent and company, and which are paid for by the agent. Find out approximately how much a new agent should budget each month.

Normally, a list like this, in much more detail, is attached to the contract you sign at affiliation. Ask to see this list during your interview, along with the contract.

The Bottom Line on Start-Up Expenses: On average, plan to spend from $2,025 to $3,150 as you begin your career.

Generally, the two largest costs are MLS fees and Realtor® dues.

Fig. 5.2   Essential Supplies and Services

Facilities and Equipment
Office space (or work from home?), copy machine, fax machine, MLS terminals, computer, printer, telephone, local calls, beverage supplies

Supplies
MLS forms (may be online), stationary, listing presentation, buyer's presentation, marketing materials

Signage
For sale signs, posts, open house signs, sold by signs

Support Services
Answering service

Access to Advertising
Newspapers, magazines, other media

Errors and Omissions Insurance

Education
Initial training, advanced training

Technology
Internet, your web site, monthly fees

Agent's Personal Promotion
Brochures, stamps, business cards, mailing/bulk mail flyers

When you interview with various companies, get a list of probable initial and ongoing costs.

Differentiate which are costs of any real estate company, and which are specific costs at that company. Find out which are additional fees.

Tools of the Trade

Your Car—Your Second Office: Typically, REALTORS® drive 15,000 to 25,000 miles a year. Truly, their second office is their car.

REALTORS* say having a comfortable, reliable car is important. Because most real estate salespeople both list and sell homes they need large enough car to show homes to a family of four. Successful buyers' agents know how important it is to make clients comfortable as they look at homes.

As a new real estate agent, I had a sports car, which I drove to work only when I had no appointments to show homes. But clients would call to ask if they could see a particular home again that afternoon. I would be stuck without my 'buyer showing' car. I learned the hard way that it is difficult to qualify and work with your buyer unless you have that buyer

---

Fig. 5.3   Tools of the Trade

Briefcase
Pen/Pencil
Colored pen or pencil Hi-Liter
Calendar
Computer
Business cards, Calculator
Street map/GPS
Tape measure (100 ft)
Reference book or bookmarked in computer
Conventional loan information
FHA/VA information*
Title insurance rates*
Escrow insurance rates*
Fire insurance rates*
Staple gun/Paper clips/Staple remover
*can be stored in your computer

Car trunk
Sold signs
Tape (sticky)
Flashlight
Coveralls
Overshoes
First-aid kit

Forms (or available on the Internet/on your computer)
Purchase and sale agreements
MLS change orders
Addendum forms
Listing forms

Promotional packages
Special programs
Listing/buyer presentations
Pre-listing presentations

in your car, getting their impressions on the areas and homes as you drive and guide the tour.

You would be surprised what you learn in casual conversation. At first, when buyers do not know or trust you, they are reticent about sharing their fondest dreams with you. To sell them a home, you must know those fondest dreams. As you get to know them, and, as often happens, even get lost with them as you struggle to find those properties you previewed, you and they become "human" to one another, instead of being merely a salesperson and a buyer couple. So, leave your zippy sports car or cozy two-door at home and drive your dependable, midsize sedan, passenger van, or SUV. Of course, be sure it is sparkling clean!

What Kind of Car Should You Drive? The kind of car you choose to drive will say a lot about you. Do not appear "flashy," unless you know your clients will feel comfortable with a flashy agent; few agents can get away with it. Yes, you see those agents on TV driving luxury cars. Who do they attract? What are they saying about themselves? Is that what you want to convey? What car reflects your target audience?

Adequate Insurance Coverage: Companies require certain auto insurance coverage. When you interview with your finalist companies, find out about the auto coverage they require and check your insurance policy to be sure your coverage is adequate. Commonly, real estate companies require liability per bodily injury at $100,000/$300,000 total, and property damage at $50,000.

Ongoing Costs to Budget

Fig. 5.4 shows typical monthly costs that you must anticipate in your budget.

Fig. 5.4   Approximate Monthly Costs

Multiple Listing Service (MLS) Fees $50

Fee for receiving all the services that the multiple listing service provides. In some areas MLS and Realtor® services are combined.

Errors and Omissions Insurance $50

Fees for insurance lawsuits; companies may "self-insure" or buy an insurance policy; check with the companies you interview with to find out the kind of insurance they provide. [including costs, limits and the deductible you will share]

Promotional $50-$200

Costs associated with marketing your listed properties: flyers, food for open houses, gifts for sellers, etc.

Miscellaneous $100

Costs associated with selling a home; gifts for buyers, etc.

Communication Costs $75-150

Cell phone charges, long-distance calls, a pager, etc.

Entertainment, Gifts $50-100

Promotion costs associated with getting and keeping customers.

Education $25-50

Continuing education, such as sales skills courses, law updates, etc.

Office Supplies $25-$75

Personal Promotion $25-$300

Promoting yourself to get new business and to keep old business, such as personal brochures, flyers, advertising.

Other Personal Promotion Expenses $200+

Personalized for sale signs, personalized name for use on for sale signs, personalized open house signs.

Realtors®: What They Spend in Expenses per Year

According to the latest National Association of REALTORS®' survey, the median amount agents laid out in business expenses was $5330 (on a gross median income of $43,300).

Tracking and Recording Your Expenses

There are several apps to help you track and record expenses. Look in apps for 'track business expenses': ExpenseTracker is one. Another is Trail wallet, which is useful to use on trips.

You will need to record your mileage, too. MileIQ Is an app for that.

Use a program such as Quickbooks® to record and track your expenses. Create a system for keeping track of your deductions. I use an accordion folder marked with each expense category. Or, you can take a picture of your receipts and store them in a software program. Software allows you to capture expenses in categories. Each time you spend money for one of the following items, record the expense in your financial program and save the receipt in the file in the correct category. Work with your accountant or take a course for independent contractors. The good news is that most of these expenses are tax-deductible, as shown in Fig. 5.5.

Fig. 5.5 Tax-Deductible Expenses	
Use a program such as Quicken® to record and track your expenses. Create a system for keeping track of your deductions (I use an accordion folder marked with each expense category). Each time you spend money for one of the following items, record the expense in your financial program and save the receipt in the file. Work with your accountant or take a course for independent contractors.	
Car	**Stationery and Supplies**
Gas, parking fees, tolls, repairs, milage	Postcards, pencils, pens, paper, film, postage, shipping

Fig. 5.5   Tax-Deductible Expenses (cont'd)

Dues and Fees

Realtor® dues, MLS, designations

Entertainment

Meals/tickets for events, advertising

Education

Continuing education, meetings, conventions, subscriptions

Books and Other Deliveries

Educational CDs, DVDs, books

Office Expenses

Secretarial/assistant

Telephone and Cell Phone

% of service, long distance, credit card calls, answering service/machine/pager

Marketing

Newspaper ads, flyers, newsletters, brochures, business cards, online

Travel and Transportation

Hotel/motel, taxis, car rental, meals, incidentals

Professional Tools

Tape recorder, tape measure, camera, calculator, adding machine, computer, computer software, printer, PDA/ Smartphone, scanner

Gifts and Supplies

Housewarmings

Moneyspire, Mint, Freshbooks, and QuickBooks Pro® are convenient computer programs many agents use to set up budgets, generate profit and loss statements, and keep track of their expenses for business management and taxes.

The costs associated with selling real estate can vary greatly, depending on the materials and services provided by your office, your dedication and desire to build your career fast and your ability to dedicate resources and dollars to your best sources of business.

Caveat: Gross is not net! Agents are lured by 100% or high commission splits. They don't realize the more money they gross, the more it is up to them to budget and allocate for their expenses with an expert eye.

What Income Do You Need to Pay your Expenses each Month?

To get an idea of your total expenses, complete the worksheet (Fig. 5.6) to figure your other normal monthly living expenses.

Fig. 5.6 Determine Your Normal Monthly Living Expenses	
House Payment or Rent	$_____
Condominium Fees	$_____
Food	$_____
Credit Cards	$_____
Entertainment, Gifts	$_____
Savings	$_____
Dental, Medical	$_____
Car (payment, gasoline, insurance, repair)	$_____
Property Taxes and Insurance	$_____
Utilities	$_____
Incidentals	$_____
Clothing	$_____
School Costs	$_____
Health, Life Insurance	$_____
Donations, Church	$_____
Miscellaneous	$_____
Total Monthly Costs	$_____

How to Establish a Budget: Your Expenses for the First Six Months

Look at those expenses as they accrue each month to see how much you will be spending during your first six months in the business. A new agent's expenses are approximately $300-$700 per month. In addition, you will need to know your personal monthly expenses to find the total you will need each month as you start your real estate career.

How much in savings will you need? On average, it will take you three to six months to get your first paycheck if you use a proven business start-up plan. (It may take you much longer to get that check if you sit and wait for that wonderful client to find you). This is where you heed Jerry's advice.

Here is a formula to compute your total first six months' expenses.

How Long to a Paycheck?

Jerry gave great advice at the beginning of this chapter. Experienced salespeople enter real estate every day. If they transfer their lead-generating skills, they begin doing the business-generating activities in great numbers on the first day of their real estate careers. Still, it takes them a few months to get their first paycheck. Using the career-oriented person as a model, let's track the amount of time it will take a careerist to generate a first sale and then a first paycheck.

Fig. 5.7 Total Money Required First 6 Months	
Your Estimated Start-Up Expenses:	$_____
Your Estimated Real Estate Expenses Monthly x 6:	$_____
Your Other Monthly Living Expenses x 6:	$_____
TOTAL MONEY REQUIRED*:	$_____

Total money required (either savings or income) for your first six months in real estate.

When Will I Get Paid?

Most agents want to get a paycheck fast. In fact, a majority of newer agents I surveyed expected to get a paycheck within the first three months. To do that, you must start lead generating in the week you're licensed. The "best case" scenario: You start lead generating for buyers in that first week. You find a buyer in the first month in the business. You "close" the sale at the end of month two.

Here's how the activities leading to your paycheck would play out through time. The will-be successful agent, you, contact hundreds of potential prospects the first month to find several qualified buyers.

You've studied the National Association of Realtor* statistics. On average, buyers look for homes for ten weeks. You also know that you must put buyers in your car eight times (just the law of averages), to sell someone a home. (That means you show homes to various people at least eight times to expect one sale from someone.)

So, you lead generate heavily, and find four buyers to work with immediately. You qualify these buyers by using a professional consultation process before putting them in your car. You prioritize them according to urgency to buy. You show homes eight times in four weeks. You sell one home at the end of your first month in the business.

It takes one to two months to "close" a home, that is, to finalize the sale and get the proceeds from the sale available to the seller.

See figure 5.8 for sales cycle time frames.

 Ask your interviewer what the average commission is per sale in that area, so you can project these numbers more accurately for your situation.

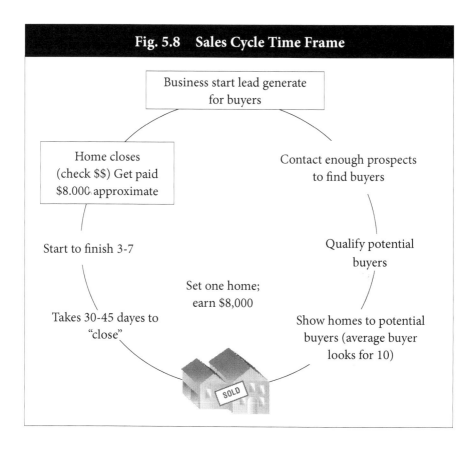

Fig. 5.8   Sales Cycle Time Frame

Business start lead generate for buyers

Home closes (check $$) Get paid $8.000 approximate

Contact enough prospects to find buyers

Start to finish 3-7

Qualify potential buyers

Set one home; earn $8,000

Takes 30-45 dayes to "close"

Show homes to potential buyers (average buyer looks for 10)

*find out the average commission for your area

Ca-ching! You get the commissions due to you when proceeds are available to the seller. Funds are dispersed to the real estate companies and your company pays you. So, you receive your first paycheck at the end of month two (again, this is a best-case scenario). In your office, the average commission to you is $10,000. (This is not a national average. It is just chosen as an example). Ask your interviewer for averages in your area.

When Will You Break Even?

From studying earning patterns and expenses of starting careerists, I have found that business expenses and income reach break-even at about month six or seven. That means checks the agent receives by the end of this period will pay for the business expenses accrued from all those months. Continuing this earning pattern, the careerist will, at the end of the year, have been paid enough generally to cover all personal and business expenses, and establish an earning pattern that will propel him or her into successful second and third years.

Your Business Multiplies Itself as You Gain Sales Skills and Contacts: You, as a new agent, are learning new sales skills and contacting more people while getting comfortable with the operations and information about real estate. The number of people you can work with at one time will increase through the months. It is uncommon, though, for even a new dedicated careerist to generate enough prospects to sell more than one home the first month or two in the business. The business multiplies as you gain skills and contacts.

In addition to the sale, this dedicated new agent finds several prospects who want to *sell*. In the second month, you list a property at a marketable price that will sell within reasonable time, which, in the careerist's area, is 30 days. Fortunately, the listed property *does* sell in 30 days. The home closes one month after the sale is finalized.

Now, it is seven months into the agent's career. Again, the commission to the agent is $10,000.

When You'll Get Paid for your Listing

Look at Fig. 5.9, where time frames are attached to the listing version of the sales cycle. From the time frames involved in selling and listing real estate, you can see why new agents are advised to sell homes for the fastest income.

Early Dumb Luck

Have you heard about an agent who sold a home at an open house his first week in the business?

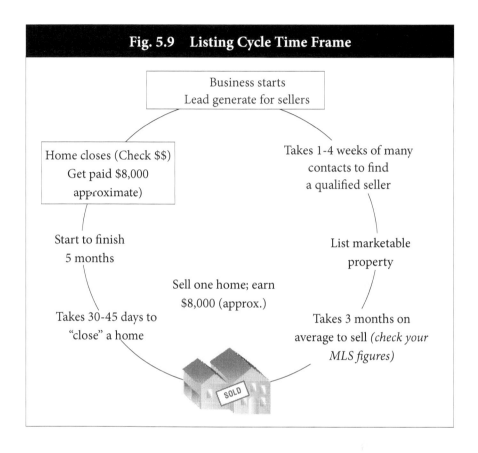

Fig. 5.9   Listing Cycle Time Frame

Business starts
Lead generate for sellers

Takes 1-4 weeks of many
contacts to find
a qualified seller

List marketable
property

Takes 3 months on
average to sell *(check your
MLS figures)*

Sell one home; earn
$8,000 (approx.)

Takes 30-45 days to
"close" a home

Start to finish
5 months

Home closes (Check $$)
Get paid $8,000
approximate)

SOLD

I call that dumb luck. Still, let's use that scenario to plan when you would get your first check. You meet a buyer at an open house during your first week. This buyer wants to buy that home and can close the transaction in 30 days. You write the offer to purchase and it's accepted. The transaction closes in 30 days, so you receive your check at the end of your second month.

Let's get serious! How often does that actually happen? Not enough to count on it. I held hundreds of homes open during my six years of sales. Once—only once—I sold that particular home to buyers who came into that open house. If it were that easy, everyone in real estate sales would either be rich—or working for a lot fewer dollars per sale!

> As you sit and listen to the interviewer sell you on her company, listen "between the lines."
>
> Is this interviewer making it sound as though all you have to do is to join that particular office and company and good things will happen for you? Or is she explaining how she will assist you in your business start- up plan, so you can be in control of your own destiny?

A Set-Up for Failure: I found in my study of new agents that the largest group (already hired and in training class) expected to receive a check by their third month in the business. However, few of them knew the work it took to assure that this happened. They did not know how many prospects they needed to contact, how many times they needed to show homes, or even how much a sale was worth.

I think they believed that, armed with a real estate license, information, a great company affiliation, and business cards, they were qualified to sell a home—and would sell one quickly.

From watching new agents' behavior, it seems they think buyers and sellers will magically find them. If that happens early in their careers (that dumb luck), they just sit and wait until the next time. Finally, their money runs out and they leave the business.

Paychecks Need to Come Quickly to Stay in Business

The newer agents I surveyed did not know the activities it took to assure their goals. In addition, they also had limited resources for staying in the business long enough to get a paycheck. On average, new REALTORS® could only stay in the business four months without a paycheck. That means they needed an aggressive business start-up plan focused on the right lead-generating activities. They needed to implement it from the first day in the office.

If managers knew new agents' expectations for early success and the need for a paycheck in those first few months, they would manage new agents differently. Instead of leaving new agents to their own devices, or at most, managers would coach new agents frequently with an effective business start-up plan. They would set up a coaching/accountability schedule, and coach that new agent to quick success—before the money runs out.

Success in your First Year

The will-be successful careerist's first goal as he or she goes into real estate is to generate hundreds of qualified prospects. He or she realizes that some of these prospects will not be buyers or sellers for months or years. This results in selling more properties consistently as the months go by. He or she lists more and more properties, which begin to sell.

Realizing his business is gathering steam, the careerist generates an increasing number of transactions. By the end of the first year, the careerist has built a solid foundation for a great career. Typically, following the careerist pattern, an agent makes $80,000 to $80,000-$100,000+ her first year. Look at the timeline (Fig. 5.10) to see how this career grows at the end of the first year.

Fig. 5.10 Careerist Timeline					
Months 1	2	3	4	5	6
7	8	9	10	11	12
Revenue units* 1	1	1	1	1	1
			1	1	2

*A revenue unit is a sale or a listing sold and is worth $10,000+ for a new agent in this sample. The careerist has established a solid foundation for a growing career by closing at least 10 transactions his first year in real estate.

How Many Sales Is Enough to Create a Great Business?

How many transactions in an agent's first year would be adequate to build a superstar career? When I ask agents that question, they usually estimate 12-24. From that, I know they have *no idea* how many transactions the average Realtor® completes. (According to a recent NAR survey, that number is ten—for REALTORS® *all years* in the business.)

After I get that 12-24 figure, I ask the new agents for minimum expectations to build a career. They settle on twelve. I think that's a good number, because it's enough to create sources of referral business, to keep your self-esteem high, and keep you going through the rough spots, to help you get really good at selling real estate, and to learn how to provide superior customer service.

The Minimum You Can Complete to Build a Business

I think it takes more than six transactions in a year to create impetus for a greater business, business ultimately built on referrals. Less than six transactions means the agent hasn't learned a lot, and, more importantly, hasn't made enough people happy fast enough to grow his business via referrals. So, shoot for at least six.

You've Got 'em, Now, How Are You Gonna Keep Them? Fig. 5.11 shows how happy buyers and sellers multiply your chances of building a powerful business in years two and three if you stay in contact with them. Marketing advice to will-be superstars:

Treat the old customer like the appreciating asset he or she is.

Smart agents create marketing plans directed precisely at past clients, so they can reap more business from their best sources: Those sellers and buyers who already think the agent is wonderful! You can see why focusing on units, not commission dollars, is key to building a strong career. Units, happy clients, refer you to more clients.

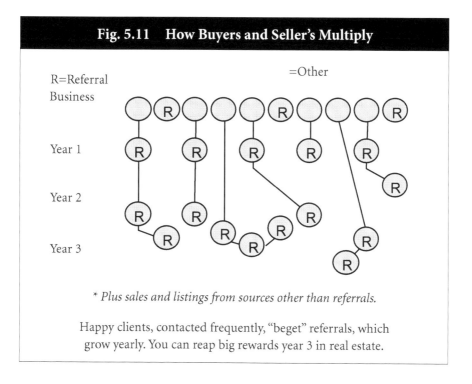

Fig. 5.11   How Buyers and Seller's Multiply

R=Referral Business

=Other

Year 1

Year 2

Year 3

* Plus sales and listings from sources other than referrals.

Happy clients, contacted frequently, "beget" referrals, which grow yearly. You can reap big rewards year 3 in real estate.

Summary

This chapter itemizes the start-up and ongoing costs for real estate agents. Important principles in this chapter are:

- Initial costs vary greatly with area and company.
- Ongoing costs vary greatly by company and are related to the company's commission splits, desk fees, and additional monthly fees.
- Even though the will-be successful careerist does the kind and amount of activities that generate income early in his or her career, certain time frames are still associated with prospecting payoffs, the buyers' decision-making process, the property time

on market, and closing. These time frames result in a commission for the new agent, at the earliest, in month two or three of his or her career.

- It is important that the new agent plan to have four to six months' income in savings to provide enough time to generate business. Unfortunately, many people enter real estate to "give it a try," with no idea of the expenses or time frames involved in beginning a career. Their money runs out before they can enjoy reaping the rewards of their lead generating work.

Even though you should have four to six months of savings to begin your real estate career, do not wait around for "something good to happen." You will become discouraged and unmotivated. By developing and implementing an aggressive business start-up plan, you can ensure that you will get a paycheck early, to be followed by an ever-growing career.

Big Ideas from Chapter 5

- You should have four to six months of savings to launch a successful career.
- You will break even at about month six if you are on a "careerist" path.
- Make your personal budget and business budget. Add your start-up and ongoing costs, to assure you have enough money saved to get you through these first four to six months.
- During your interview, get a list of start-up and office expenses from each office. Be sure you understand what those expenses mean to you and what they get for you.
- It will take about eight to twelve transactions your first year to build a credible foundation for a return and referral business. Get to critical mass as fast as you can!

Get a Jump-Start on Success

- Choose software for your financial record-keeping as you begin the business.

- Get an accountant. Meet with your accountant to set up your financial software and discuss how you're going to keep detailed records.

- Figure your start-up costs and check to assure you have them.

- Compute your monthly costs and check to assure you have four to six months of savings to support you while you begin this new career.

- Make a personal budget if you don't have one.

- Make a rough business budget so you will know the expenses you'll have each month, using the guide here.

CHAPTER 6

What It Takes
to Get a Real Estate License

"Get your pre-license training from a reputable real estate training school. Don't think, though, that the course fully prepares you to sell real estate. The pre-license training does not prepare you adequately for face-to-face contact with clients—a skill that is essential to success."

~Connie Walsh, top 10 percent of her company, former chef

In This Chapter

- Requirements for Becoming Licensed
- What Kind of School Should I Attend?
- The Real Estate Exam—Tips to Pass the First Time
- Time Frame: From Course to Licensing
- How to Prepare Now to 'Hit the Ground Running'
- Big Ideas
- Get a Jump-Start to Success

You have been considering a career in real estate. You think you fit the profile. You understand the requirements. So far, you are still in the game. You love the thought of being independent, and you are excited about the challenge and responsibility of creating your own business and your own income. You have calculated the amount of savings you'll need. What is next? Gaining a real estate license.

Requirements for Becoming Licensed

Agencies Responsible for Licensing Regulations

Each of the 50 states, and each of the provinces of Canada has some type of governmental agency responsible for the administration of real estate license laws. This agency makes rules regarding real estate practice, enforces laws governing real estate licensees, and sets criteria, including educational standards, for pre-licensing and post-licensing requirements.

The real estate licensing agencies' duty is to protect the public interest. These agencies are all a part of the Association of Real Estate Law Officials (ARELLO), a federation of law officials created to assist each other in the administration and enforcement of license laws in the United States and Canada. Since ARELLO's inception in 1930, a major accomplishment has been to develop uniform legislation to better protect the consuming public.

Some states' agencies incorporate education directors, education advisory committees, and an education research center or fund. The trend is toward increasing pre-license and post-license requirements.

The requirements to get your real estate license:

- Must meet minimum age requirements (18 in most states and provinces).
- Must pay an exam and licensing fee, which ranges from approximately $150 to $300, depending on the state (license good for one to four years, depending on the state or province).
- Must take and pass a licensing exam.

Educational Requirements: More than three-fourths of states and provinces require the completion of certain real estate courses. These range from "home study" to 90 or more hours of completed class time. In some locations, applicants must show proof of completing specific, prescribed courses before taking the exam. These courses prepare applicants to take and pass the exam. In addition, some areas waive part or all of the educational requirements if the applicant has equivalent experience, such as a real estate license in another state, or a law degree.

Information About Licensing Requirements Available from ARELLO: The licensing fees, term of the license, and pre- licensing and post-licensing educational requirements around the world are available online from ARELLO (www.arello.com), the Association of License Law Officials. There may be a fee for this information.

Another good reference is Kaplan Real Estate Education. They are a large national real estate school, offering pre-license and post-licensing courses throughout the U S. Many of the schools you see advertised are re-sellers for the Kaplan courses. See the information on the state in which you want to practice. You will find licensing requirements, steps to get licensed, and more.

Note: There is lots of information on becoming a real estate agent on the Kaplan site. Personally, I have some differences of opinion with some of the advice offered there. You will see what I mean as you read Kaplan's opinions and mine. My advice comes from interviewing hundreds of would-be agents, training them, and observing why some make it in this business—and some do not.

Questions to Ask Your Licensing Agency: Your state or provincial licensing agency will provide you with the information you need regarding the specific requirements for your location. Each state or province has a Web site, where you can download and print the latest requirements, or you can call or email your government licensing agency for a publication (and look at their sites online). Here are the things you need to find out:

- Age requirement
- Pre-license education hours required: How many, within what time period
- Which schools teach the courses and how the courses are delivered
- Cost of license fee and the term of the license
- Study materials available and where to purchase and costs
- How to apply for the exam
- Where/when are exams given
- Re-exam available? How to apply/cost
- How to apply for a license
- Other licensing requirements—waivers
- Pass-fail rates of various schools

How to Study for the Exam: A few states and provinces do not require the completion of approved courses before taking the licensing exam. However, for most people with rusty study habits and conflicting commitments, I recommend taking a course to prepare you to pass.

Exam Study Guides: Each U.S. state and Canadian province publishes a study guide, usually in conjunction with their testing service. When you call or email the regulatory agency, ask if a study guide is available. In addition, books are available to help you study for your exam.

What Kind of School Should I Attend?
College Courses

With the constant escalation of pre-license requirements, all kinds of schools have leaped into the real estate education business. State and community colleges have courses to prepare you to pass the exam. Of all the courses available, these courses generally have the longest time frame, extending throughout the term or semester. If you like plenty of reflection time and class time, a state or community college is probably a good choice. Usually these courses are of good quality and are taught by knowledgeable instructors. Choose an instructor who keeps the course on track—or you will not get enough drill in memorization to pass the exam the first time.

Private Real Estate Schools

As states and provinces continue to increase the educational pre- license requirements, more privately owned schools have sprung up to fill the need. Sometimes affiliated with real estate companies, they are called proprietary schools. Many of these schools exist just to provide pre- licensing courses. Most of these schools are re-sellers of large education providers, such as Kaplan Real Estate Education. You may be able to see the schools registered in various states, and what they offer, by going to your Department of Licensing real estate division. In my state of Washington, I'm able to see all the schools approved to teach clock-hour courses, and the courses they provide.

If you are looking for a "live" course, search online for "Real Estate School."

A caution about "live" courses: Sometimes students take over the class, asking the instructor many "interesting" questions that are not pertinent to the course. The reason you are there is to prepare to pass the exam.

Questions to Ask the School: To be an accredited real estate school, the school and its administrator must meet certain requirements of the state regulatory agency. Generally, those requirements are minimal. As you can imagine, schools range from maybe OK to excellent. Check out the school before paying your money. Call, visit or check online and find out what type of course delivery is offered. Choose the study program that best fits your needs. Here are questions to ask:

- What is the length of the program?
- Who are the teachers?

- With whom is the school affiliated?
- What is the school's test "pass" rates, if available? (In some states, schools aren't allowed to publish or publicize these.)
- Who is the provider of the curriculum? (Most proprietary schools contract with a provider, like Kaplan, to re-sell the course). Ask to see the course curriculum and materials. Find out what the fee includes. Ask if there is an additional fee for a "cram" course before the exam.
- Get recommendations from the school's students.

Type of Study Programs

Here is a synopsis of the two most popular delivery methods of pre-license courses today.

Live Lecture: The live lecture usually takes six to thirteen weeks to complete, and is in lecture format, with one or more live instructors. If you are the kind of person who likes to learn with others, this format is for you. Lecture format is used in college programs and some private proprietary schools.

In addition, some private schools offer classroom format in "cram" courses. You will get lots of information verbally, but you must also study on your own to assimilate and memorize it. Group discussion can be interesting but can get you off track, for there may be licensed agents in the live class who are studying for their brokers' exams.

Interactive Computer Programs: These programs are online. You sign up online or by phone or mail with the school and can take the course at your computer on your own time. The computer keeps track of the number of hours you spend studying. You will get a workbook and will take sample tests.

If you like working on your own, you may want to investigate this type of program. Because these courses focus mainly on helping you memorize the material on the exam, students who take them enjoy a high pass rate.

About that Real Estate Exam

All 50 states and the Canadian provinces require an exam before licensing. These exams are given regularly throughout the year in various testing sites. Generally, the licensee's exam is about four hours in length. Each state's test is divided into two areas:

- National material covering areas common to all states and provinces (financing, contracts, brokerage, valuation, and ownership)
- Local material covering areas specific to that state or province (rules, regulations, laws, procedures)

The Nature of the Test Questions: There are about 100 questions on a licensing exam. All of the test questions are multiple choice; they ask the applicant to recall definitions, laws, and licensing rules and to compute simple real estate math problems. In most states, a passing grade is 70 to 75 percent. Some states combine the scores of both sections of the exam. In others, applicants must pass each section, but may take only one section again if they fail a particular section.

Math: About 20 to 25 percent of the questions on the exam will require some math. This fact strikes fear in the hearts of many readers. Not to worry. This math is basic arithmetic, about the level you studied in the 6th to 8th grade. However, if you feel shaky about this area (and it's common to feel that way), take a business math, basic math, or math review course at your community college.

Ace That Exam

Proven Study Tips: The real estate exam is a means to control the number of applicants into the field. The exam questions deal with some pretty esoteric material. In fact, even seasoned real estate agents admit they would have to take a course again to pass the test because they don't use that information in everyday real estate!

I know some of you reading this feel the same way about tests as I feel about needles! So, here are some tips from a real estate agent (me) who long ago figured out how to study for and pass tests.

Six Study Tips and Why They Work

Before each in-class session, or when you start your next online chapter, skim the new chapter for highlights. Then, read the chapter carefully. You need to get the "big picture" before you grasp the details. This is "the forest and the trees" study truism: "You can't see the forest for the trees." When you use this study tip, you will see both when you need to.

Learning Fact: Experts tell us we "learn what we already know." In other words, you must have a *context* for what you are learning. By seeing the big picture first, you have context. Then, you fill in the blanks with the details. Works every time... I promise.

Right after class, review your class subjects and notes. Why? We remember only ten percent of what we've heard three days after we heard it.

Learning Fact: We learn through repetition. You will need to revisit each concept at least six times to commit it to memory.

Make a notebook (hard copy or online) with all the definitions you covered in each class session. Create test questions to match words and definitions.

Learning Fact: It takes time and repetition to make that learning stick long-term. Now you are making your learning go deeper. You are rearranging it so you really grasp it.

If you learn through listening, and you can't listen to audio only, record yourself saying the definitions. Play these in your car as you drive.

Learning Fact: Use all the senses to learn. Seeing, hearing, and *using* the material increases your retention to 65 percent three days later.

Keep up with the class work. Faithfully attend every session and study every chapter. Study regularly between sessions. If you have ever gotten behind on your work in school, you know why this is important!

Take every practice exam until you are comfortable with the process and format.

Learning Fact: When you are successful doing something, your fear goes away, and you look forward to doing that again. Train yourself to win!

Taking the Test: Face it. We have all had exam anxiety at some time. Here are five pointers that will help you relax, control your emotions, and pass the test the first time you take it:

- Read each question slowly; then, read all the possible answers. Do not jump to conclusions to mark the "right" answer. Instead, tell yourself why each answer is wrong. By the process of elimination, find the only answer you think is correct. If you find two out of four that may be correct, leave that question and come back to it.

- Remember, the point of the exam is to limit the number of agents coming into the field. One of the ways to do this is to write exams where exam takers jump to the "right" answer. Do not fall for it!

- Do not answer any questions unless you are absolutely sure of the answer. Skip questions for which you are unsure and come back to them. You will either remember the answer later as you "warm up," or the remaining questions will give you some hints as to the other answers.

- Take your time. You will have plenty of time to answer each question on the exam.

- Build your self-confidence as you start by skimming the exam. Find some questions you are certain you can correctly answer and answer them first. Amazingly, when your mind gets warmed up, you will find you can think through questions that baffled you when you tried to attack them at the beginning of the testing period.

- Let the test give you the answers. By reading through the complete test first, answering only the questions you are sure of, you will find hints of other answers. Your confidence will soar, and you will find you are answering more questions as the test period continues.

What If You Do Not Pass the First Time? All states and provinces allow you to pay a reexamination fee and take all or part of the exam again. Some states have no limit on the number of times you can retake the exam; other states have limits of three to twelve times. In states that divide the test into two sections, you will probably be able to retake only the part of the exam you failed.

General Passing Rates: Ratios of students passing the exam range widely from state to state. No matter what the rate, the important consideration for you is that it always builds more confidence to pass any exam the first time.

What Passing the Exam Means: The content and format tests the applicant's level of knowledge concerning memorized facts, rules, and laws. The applicant can answer multiple-choice questions correctly, which proves he has accumulated lists of facts, rules and laws in his mind at least for the short term. Remember, this exam principally serves as a screening device for regulatory agencies, to control the number of new licensees who enter the field each year.

Doesn't Passing the Test Predict Success in Real Estate? Simply, no. Success (making money) in real estate depends on what you do, not what you know. It depends on having the tenacity, determination, and focus to self-start and keep going through more objections than you ever thought possible. People who are successful in real estate are those who understand it is a "people" business, not a "memorizing facts" business.

From Exam to First Day in the Business

If your state requires the completion of a course to prepare you to take the exam, much of your time frame is set by the particular course you choose. As mentioned earlier, the term or semester program at a college will be the longest format. The self-directed programs will be relatively the shortest. Check the laws of your state or province and the availability of various course formats.

On average, plan on at least three weeks of study to prepare for your licensing exam. Be sure to check the application procedures in your state. Generally, states require that you apply to take the exam days to weeks before an exam date. However, because exams are now online, you may be able to register for the exam and take it that same day. Fig. 6.1 provides a timeline, so you can see approximate time frames, from the time you start your research to the field to the time you affiliate with a company.

When Will I Get My Exam Results? In states that test online, you will receive notice you passed the exam right on the spot. In other states, you will know within about two weeks after your exam date. With those results in hand, you may affiliate with a broker, send your application to the state (with your broker's signature), and be eligible to sell real estate.

Note: In Washington state, where I live, you are not approved to sell real estate until your background check and fingerprints have been processed. This takes about two to four weeks after you pass your test. Check your state to see the specific time frame requirements.

Fig. 6.1   Timeline - From Interest to Affiliation

Pre-interview (with managers to find out more about field)

▶10 Sign up to take per-license course

▶10 Send fee to state to take real estate exam

▶10 Attend course on real estate as your business 40

▶10 Start Hit the Ground Running Activity Plan 40

▶12 Completed interviews with 3 to 5 real estate companies 45

➡ Begin real estate pre-license study

▶15 Attend sales skill building workshop 45

▶30 Take exam (depends on state's educational requirements) 90

▶ 90 Get exam results 105

0 1 2 3 4 5 6 7 8 9 10 11 12 13 14 15   30   90   100   105

Days

Overall, plan a time frame of at least four weeks minimum from the time you begin studying for your exam to the time you are licensed, and that's a minimum time frame.

Other Licensing Requirements

Most states require continuing education (CE) requirements to maintain a real estate sales license. These requirements range from three hours every year to 60 or more hours every two years. Generally, the subjects approved for license renewal are technical in nature:

- Law updates
- Finance
- Environmental issues

Some states spell out specific courses required and even include curriculum. Some states require an ethics course. Through requiring licensees to learn the facts regarding these topics, regulatory agencies can fulfill their charge to "protect the public interest." Because of the increasing number of laws, rules, and regulations, keeping licensees up to date through continuing education is a large concern of regulatory agencies today.

For your state's requirements, contact your state's regulatory agency. The managers you interview with can also tell you the continuing licensing requirements in your area.

How to Prepare Now to Hit the Ground Running

Passing the exam does not guarantee you will be successful selling real estate. So, what can you do while you are studying to literally *hit the ground running* after you are licensed? Use my checklist, *30 Things to Do Now to Hit the Ground Running* (Appendix C and on my website). You can prepare now, get organized, practice sales skills, and gather important information. I have also put this checklist on my website. (In fact, when you order this eBook through me, you receive this checklist with the eBook).

You are prepared. Having accomplished so much, you will be ready to find, work with, and sell homes from the first day you are licensed. You will avoid that horrible time-eating syndrome, getting ready to get ready, that new agents experience. They are overwhelmed with a myriad of tasks and can easily get lost in them. I have worked with many agents with *Hit the Ground Running* implemented during their pre-license study, I have seen how much better they do when they've completed that *Hit the Ground Running* checklist prior to getting licensed.

Summary

This chapter discusses licensing requirements, study tips, and post-license education and training. Important ideas are:

- Passing the pre-license exam does not prepare you to sell real estate nor is it a predictor of your success in real estate.

- The pre-license curriculum and test format may mislead agents to assume that success in real estate sales is directly related to the accumulation of facts, definitions, and laws regarding real estate.

- Get information about selling real estate from sources other than a pre-license course. These sources include educational courses, skill-developing workshops, career nights, and books about selling real estate.

Big Ideas from Chapter 6

- Choose the pre-license course best suited to how you like to learn.
- Apply the study lessons here so you pass the test the first time around.

Get a Jump-Start on Success

- Research the courses available to you.
- Contact your state to find out licensing requirements in that state.
- Make a timeline to plan your course registration, study time frame, and license test date.
- Register for the course—you are off to the races!
- Implement 30 Things to Do During Pre-License Training to Hit the Ground Running (appendix C)

CHAPTER 7

Finding the Right Real Estate Office for You

"As a broker, I heard this question frequently from newly licensed agents: How much do you charge? That's the wrong question. The right question is how much will I make and how will you help me do that?"

~ Brian Leavitt, former real estate owner, designated broker, top producer, Issaquah, Wa.

In This Chapter

- When to Start Your Search for a Real Estate Office
- Which Type of Company Is Best for You?
- How to Research Companies and Offices in Your Area
- Evaluate the Companies You Prefer
- Big Ideas
- Get a Jump-Start to Success

Often, agents choose an office because:

- "It's close to home."
- "The desk fee was small."
- "They said they'd train me."
- "It was a small office."
- "The broker said I could work as her assistant for a while."
- "They promised me 'leads.'"

Guess what? These are all the wrong reasons. After six months of failure the agent realizes that he or she did not do the research that should have been done to find out what was important to personal success in a search for a real estate office.

Here is another "10" on that honesty scale: I'm going to offend some brokers who try to sell agents on benefits that really don't assure success, such as "big is good," or "small is good," or "we supply leads." At the same time, brokers thank me for telling the whole story. These brokers would rather hire agents who know the pros and cons of the business before they commit to a career in real estate.

When to Start Your Search for a Real Estate Office

You are serious about a career in real estate. You have done some investigation of pre-license programs and worked on the time frames involved in studying for and taking your pre-license test. You may have already talked to some real estate companies in your area. Your next step is to gather more information about companies and offices in your area.

Ideally, you will want to do this while you are studying for your licensing exam. Then, as you near your test date, you can begin your interviews with specific offices and managers. That way, by the time you have your exam results in hand, you will have completed most of the process of choosing the right company, office, and manager for you. If you have already taken and passed your real estate exam, you can start investigating companies and offices right away. Take your time in making your decision. It is the most important one you will make regarding your real estate career.

Which Type of Company Is Best for You?

Years ago, prospective agents merely walked down the street to their well-known, independent local broker-manager-owner, chatted a while, and "hired on." The new agent understood that the image of the company was created and perpetuated by that broker-owner. He understood that affiliating with that company suggested that he, too, projected that image. Also, the agent was usually assured of being mentored by that broker-owner. With few franchises to choose from, choosing a real estate company was a local issue, and agents generally chose the company because they liked the broker and/or the office was located close to where they lived.

Now, the picture has changed. While a majority of real estate companies are not franchised, they consist mainly of small companies with fewer than twenty people. About 53 percent of REALTORS® are affiliated with an independent company. Forty-two percent of all REALTORS® are affiliated with a company that is, in turn, affiliated with a regional or national franchise, because the larger the company, the more likely it is a member of a franchise.

Franchise Affiliation and Your Income: Do you think you will make more money affiliating with a franchise? There are pros and cons to any affiliation.

The Battle of the Affiliations

Here is some background so you will have some perspective on how we got to where we are today. This will help you when you start hearing all those wonderful company stories as you interview.

Fifty years ago, most real estate companies were independent, with no local, regional, or national affiliations. Generally, a new real estate company sprang up when a good salesperson got tired of working for someone else and said, "I should start my own shop. I'm a good salesperson, and I might as well keep the whole commission." Real estate companies were generally "mom-and-pop shops," run by good salespeople, some of whom were good businesspeople—and some, not so much. It's still true that competent salespeople decide to start their own companies. This is generally how independent firms start.

The Franchise Idea Meets Real Estate: As franchising became popular in many businesses in the 1970s, it was inevitable that this idea would be translated to real estate. What a wonderful idea to capture and control all those small, independent real estate businesses to imbue the consistency of a McDonald's into these mom-and-pop real estate companies. Early franchisees saw benefits. They could get the business services they needed to compete in an increasingly sophisticated market, and they could unite in a single identity nationally for vastly increased market recognition and advertising power.

Challenges to National Franchises: As these franchises gained momentum, many real estate practitioners in the 70's predicted that this franchise idea of affiliating independent owners under one banner would rule the real estate world. The '80's and '90's showed that would not be the case.

Uniform Color Does Not Translate to Uniform Practice. One challenge to these early franchisers was that they affiliated sometimes wildly disparate owners under one set of colors. Instead of creating a stronger company image, a reason for franchising, it only changed the color of the signs in the neighborhood. It was like a neighborhood hamburger joint putting a golden arches sign out front, and trying to convince the customer it was a McDonald's®.

Franchisers based in a city thousands of miles from their franchisees found it difficult to control the image they wanted to project, especially on a national level. Brokers, being independent souls, wanted the services that the franchiser provided, but they wanted to continue to do things *their* way, even when it clashed with the franchiser image. So, this clash of images created confusion with the public.

The public did not buy the idea that adding a franchise name automatically assured the consumer better service. Finally, brokers found that, to compete in their marketplaces, they had to become better businesspeople, even with franchise benefits.

Independent Firms' Growth from Citywide to Regional: At the same time various franchises on a national level were attempting to attract the small independent broker, another trend was developing. The large independent company, dominant in its city, grew into the market region surrounding it. This type of company understood the nuances of the area and had earned a dominant market share. Because it had one leader or president, the company marketed a consistent image within its area of expertise. So, voila! Another huge player grew to dominate market share, especially in large metropolitan areas: The regional independent company.

In the past few years, the regional independent company has increased its presence in its market area by franchising to markets close by. Another method franchising companies use to grow is to buy independent companies. As you could predict from the experience of the national franchisers, some regional independents are experiencing the same image conflict. Well-prepared firms avoid these conflicts by choosing franchisees carefully, orienting new franchisees thoroughly on the image and philosophy of the company, and providing strong training programs for managers and owners.

The Large National Company: Seeing the potential to harness huge sources of revenue, the financial management community decided to leap into the breach, to capture disparate real estate companies under one umbrella. However, they did it differently. To avoid the challenges that confronted the franchisers, financial management businesses decided to buy up local independent real estate companies to create huge national companies. Then they could control the images, both in communities, and on a national level. Now, these national companies have added franchisees, independent local real estate companies who keep ownership but contract for the sales and management services this national entity provides.

In the past few years, more financial management companies have entered the real estate business this way. This is a continuing trend. As you can imagine though, that bothersome "image" problem pops up again, when companies have two or more different kinds of businesses operating under one name.

An example: ABC Realty is a national company, controlled by its corporation on the west coast. It has 100 offices nationally. It also franchises and has 300 independent owners who use the franchise services. You can see how difficult it is to portray one united company image with two different sets of operating models and 400 different owners.

Today's Affiliates: The affiliated category of real estate offices has three general arrangements:

- Franchises that own no real estate companies but provide services to independent companies.
- Regional independent companies who also franchise.
- National companies who also franchise.

Just because a firm, franchised or not, has a major market share doesn't mean you will be successful with them. Your success depends on your effort!

As you start your job search, compare the local franchises in your market area with all types of independent companies. Observe:

- "Do they convey the same image?
- Are their offices consistent in quality?
- What about their agents?
- Are there specific differences obvious with one franchise's agents from another's?"

If you are going to affiliate with a company because you like its image, be sure that it has a cohesive, not splintered image. The next chapter will give you some questions to ask the manager and agents of a particular office, so you can determine how well the company image and services are communicated and used by the agents.

Many Companies Are Not Affiliated with a Larger Entity

Many companies across the United States have chosen to remain independent. Some of the best companies around are those which have learned to compete with the giants. There is one word that describes every company that has held its own in the real estate marketing wars: Specialists. That means that a particular company has figured out what it is really good at (Its 'core competency'). It specializes in that particular product or service—or several products and services.

To focus their resources and image in the marketplace, these specialists have given up trying to be all things to all people. They do not try to do a "little of this and a little of that." Instead, they have developed sales and training programs to serve identifiable markets. Specialty areas in products include:

- Builder/developer marketing and sales
- Condominium sales
- Resale homes in certain areas and price ranges
- Waterfront properties
- Land and lot sales
- Specialty markets in consumer groups served include:
- First-time buyers
- Move up buyers
- Transferred buyers and sellers
- Retirees

To compete with large independents and franchisees, the managers of these companies have had to get really good at certain skills: Recruiting, selling, marketing promotion, and training. For the new agent, or the agent who is stuck at a certain production level, there are many benefits of affiliating with a manager who has personally developed the marketing and sales skills for success in this decade.

What About a Small Town That Has No Specialists?

As I teach courses to managers and agents around the nation, real estate practitioners from smaller market areas try to tell me that they are not specialists because their town is too small for them to specialize. However, after I chat with those who are successful, I discover they have built their businesses by becoming really good at certain things—a group of products or services.

For instance, one broker built his business by targeting repeat business in both commercial and residential real estate. To get repeat business, he built customer satisfaction programs to ensure that his customers would be so happy, they would always want to work with his agents again. He trained his agents to keep in close contact with past customers and clients to assure they were happy. He built his advertising campaigns to re-attract past customers instead of just trying to entice new ones (much more expensive and not so effective). Quite a specialist in customer satisfaction, I'd say!

Specialties can mean excelling in services as well as in products. As you consider the independent company in your area, determine the firm's specialty, how good they are at it, and whether these specialties are the ones you want to build your business around.

Which Is Better for You, an Affiliate or Non-Affiliate?

Each type of company organization has benefits for you. Each type also has drawbacks. Large companies with regional or national affiliations have training programs and marketing services that may not be available in small companies. They have money to spend on technology and personnel resources available for it. Affiliated or large companies have name recognition in wider market areas, so that the agent new to the business has the benefit of attaching his name to a recognizable company in the area.

On the Debit Side: Sometimes a new agent can get lost in a large office. Too many new agents join a big company because they think the name recognition will assure their successes. Then, they sit around waiting for something good to happen. If there is no one specifically trained and committed to teaching and coaching them in a business start-up plan, most fail. Sometimes that training is so generic and undirected it is practically useless. However, agents don't know that until it's too late. They think all training and coaching is the same.

Before you leap to an affiliated company, ask "What does this affiliation mean to me? How will I use the services available to me? No matter the size of the company or its affiliations, the most important question for you is: Who will personally invest energies daily (if needed) to ensure that I get started fast?"

 Find out what the performance expectations are for new and ex-perienced agents in each office and match your expectations accordingly. If there are no performance expectations, ask the company manager, "Why?"

What Size Office Is Best for Me?

The trend is toward offices with more salespeople, because it costs less per agent to operate a single large office than several smaller ones. Because of operating costs and generous commission splits to agents, brokers are finding it ever more challenging to make a profit. They are challenged to find a combination of agent services and reasonable profitability.

Another reason offices have gotten larger is regionalization. This means that 40 to 500+ agents work out of one office, to cover one market region. This is possible because Multiple Listing Services have combined, Realtor® associations have merged, and technology allows agents to access information in much wider areas than before (try "international").

Small Can be More Productive: Even though the trend is toward larger, regionalized offices, a recent study by the National Association of REALTORS® showed that average agent productivity was higher in a smaller office. Why? Because larger offices hire more new agents. It takes a while for new agents to be productive, and some of them get out of the business quickly, so the new agents pull down the average. Also, some offices hire many part-timers or have low producers sharing desks (or having no desk available in the office).

Who Is Absolutely Dedicated to Your Success?

Your concern, whether the office is large or small, is who is going to help you be successful. You will need people and systems to get you started. In a large office of more than 35 to 40 salespeople, you will probably need to have a coach to help you get started fast. This coach needs to be formally trained to help new agents, have a proven new agent business start-up plan, and have a systematic method to meet and counsel with you. It is not impossible, but unlikely, that the manager of a larger office has the time, singular interest, and/or expertise to devote to you those first few critical weeks and months.

Your Most Important Choice

You get the message. None of the company advantages means much unless you affiliate with an office and manager who represent the company in a way that is consistent with its overall image. None of the company features and benefits means much to you without a manager who has a business start-up plan and a coaching program so you can implement a real-life success pattern.

Rather than run yourself ragged comparing company advantages, you should spend much *more* time evaluating offices and managers. Even in the most tightly run real estate company, each office has its own persona, specialties and methods of operation. Most of the persona comes from the manager.

How to Research Companies and Offices in Your Area

As you are studying for your license, start narrowing your search for an appropriate office. By the time you are ready to take your test, you should have targeted three or four offices where you want to interview. Here are the steps to take to find those offices.

Choosing Your Market Area: The Best and Easiest for You

To be successful in today's marketing world, define a specific geographic market area where you want to work. Because building your career depends on getting known in an area as a real estate expert, confine your business to an area small enough for you to develop name recognition. Here are the best and easiest market areas for a new agent:

- Where you already have friends and business acquaintances
- Where you live, because you know the area and its businesses and its service people

Location—About Where You Live: As a manager, I watched agents attempt to start real estate careers in areas far removed from where they lived, which proved difficult. By the time they commuted a half-hour or more to their office, it was too far out of the area with which they were familiar. However, with the regionalization of real estate offices, more and more agents have home offices and travel further to their real estate office location. Ask yourself, "What affiliations and relationships do I need in order to feel a part of this organization quickly?"

Property Type: What type and price range do you want to specialize in? Do you want to help first-time buyers? Do you relate to move-up or transferred buyers? What kind of properties do these people buy? Do you own a condominium and want to specialize in them?

After deciding what type of buyers and properties you prefer, drive through the areas where these properties are located. Look at the "For Sale" signs in the area. Which companies specialize in the type of property you want to list and sell? Are there specific agents who dominate that area? Call them and talk to them about real estate, their managers, and their offices.

Why Not Specialize in High-End Properties? New agents sometimes tell me that they only want to list and sell expensive properties. They are drawn to "prestige" and "lots of commission dollars." Before you decide, look at the price range of properties that consistently sell in that area. You will likely find it's generally the low to mid-price range. The higher the price range, the longer the market time, and the fewer listings actually sell. In addition, sellers in this price range demand agents spend thousands of their own dollars in staging, pre-inspections, video tours, and glossy brochures. Finally, it takes longer to get paid—and you'll get paid fewer times.

There is lots of competition for up-market property from experienced, successful agents who have worked their way into that market over a period of years, starting when their clients were buying starter homes. The agents create return and referral business from these people.

Make lots of people happy—fast. Most importantly, new agents need to make lots of people happy their first year in the business to create powerful referral and return businesses. Although one $15,000 commission looks great, one or two happy clients per year does not help you build a dynamic referral business. (Think at least eight to twelve happy consumers your first year. Remember those 'happy revenue units'.)

Choosing an Area New to You. If you are new to town, drive around the various areas. Note the kind of homes in each area. Ask yourself, "Would my natural social circle live in these homes? Would I feel comfortable listing and selling this type of property?" New agents worry too much about not having social contacts if they're new to the area. Remember, it is not who you know; it's who you *contact consistently* that builds business.

Other Sources of Information: Contact your local Multiple Listing Service (MLS) and the local National Association of REALTORS® city or state association. The multiple listing service can give you the number of offices in the company, location of the offices, and the number of agents in a particular office. You can go on-line to the companies in your area and check the rosters of agents. Your local National Association of REALTORS® can give you additional information about offices in the area.

After choosing three or four offices or companies, query people inside and outside the business to get the kind of perspective many agents only get after they have affiliated, which is a little late.

More Methods to Research Offices

Evaluate Company Websites. Of course, I know you will go to the websites of your top four or five companies. What is the overall impression you have from seeing the site? What does it say about the company? Who is the site appealing to? Is it easy for clients to find an agent on the site? Are the agents' contact information and their websites listed on the site? Some company websites are strong on company features and/or client home searches. Some give equal weight to assisting clients in finding agents. Which do you feel is more important? Will your image complement the company site image? Does the company have a section on agent training?

Include Company Recruiting Sites. Companies or offices may also have separate recruiting sites. Some do not even name the company. If you can, find those sites and compare them with the main company site. What is your overall impression? With the information in this book, how realistic are the claims on the site?

Title Companies, Mortgage Companies, Real Estate Attorneys, Banks, and Builders: Call several people who regularly do business with these three or four real estate offices or companies for an inside view on how those offices or companies treat their clients. Ask them about the level of professionalism, the company's strengths, specialties, weaknesses, and challenges. Ask them for their recommendations and the reasons. Ask them to recommend particular managers or owners, and the reasons. Remember to ask enough people so that you do not rely on one person's opinion.

Public Open Houses: Inspect Homes and Question Agents. On Saturday or Sunday, find some "open house" signs in the area where you want to work. Just drive to the open houses in those areas and visit with agents holding houses open. Ask them how they like their offices, why they joined that office, the specialties of that office, and about their manager. Ask about the training they received. Find out the level of team cooperation and assistance from seasoned agents to new agents. Do they 'haze' new agents or give a hand up?

Check Out the Agent's Open House Strategies. This is a great tip to prepare you to hold your own open houses competitively and successfully. Note the level of professionalism that the agent demonstrates in holding the open house, both in the home's preparation and marketing, and in the agent's sales skills. As you inspect the home, ask yourself:

- Is the level of material available in the home graphically pleasing? Does it look professional? Is it created with the sales process in mind?
- Is the property staged properly for an open house? Is it clean, does it smell fresh, and is it ready for visitors? Is the exterior clean and the landscaping spruced up?
- Does the agent have the professional appearance and demeanor with which you would want to be associated? How casual is the agent about holding the open house?

Observe the agent's sales skills. Where was the agent when you entered the home? Does the agent have a list of questions for interviewing prospective buyers to get appointments, or does the conversation seem haphazard? How is the agent dealing with the potential prospects if multiple prospects are in the house?

Questions to Ask the Agent: After you have observed these things, introduce yourself. Ask if the agent has attended a sales program on open houses given by the agent's company or office. Was there practice in that sales training, or did someone just talk about how to do it, and how he or she did it? Were there processes and systems included? Was there field work, where agents inspected active open houses to evaluate best and worst methods?

The Low, Median, and the High Producer: Your sales skills, processes, and systems will likely reflect that of most of the agents in a particular office. Why? Because those are the pace, expectations, and training levels of that office. Beware of being enticed to an office where there are only a few top producers and the rest are low producers. (Where are the one-to three-year agents striving to move up?) Managers sometimes use those high producers as "bell cows" (to echo a phrase used by a fellow I once worked for). These high producers are pointed out as examples to new agents. "He did it, and you will too."

You may be told that you too, will be a top producer merely by joining the office. If that's true, then why aren't all their agents top producers? Why does the manager think you are so special? Remember, we model our careers around those agents we see every day. If you want to be successful, choose an office where there are lots of agents striving to be more successful. You want to be carried along on that tide of excellence.

Ask Clients: Ask the public about their experiences with the real estate companies on your list. Find out about their experiences with particular agents. Ask for customers' recommendations for offices and good agents. Call those agents and ask questions about their experiences.

It amazes me that real estate agents join a real estate company because they see lots of company advertising.

 Realtor® surveys show that buyers' first step in the buying process was through the Internet (44%), through a real estate agent (16%), or through a friend (6%).
Advertising accounted for less than 1 percent.

What is the Company's Image?

Gather all the paper advertising and other media on each company. Ask yourself, "From what I see, does this company know who it is? Does it project a consistent image? Do its signs, television and radio ads, mailers, and other promotional pieces speak with one voice? What impression do they want me to have about them through this advertising? Does the company image match what I want to project?"

 Don't think that company advertising is going to get you many "leads." Advertising is mainly an appeasement for sellers who like to see their ads in the paper, and to communicate that company is large and rich enough to advertise. (This would be image or institutional advertising.)

Evaluate the Companies You Prefer

Now, put all your impressions of the company together: its agents, the perceptions of its customers, its product and image advertising, and its perceived persona. How do they add up? Can you see yourself in this company? Use. Figure 7.1 to capture your evaluation.

Fig. 7.1 Evaluation Checklist	
Affiliations	
☐ None	☐ National
☐ Regional	☐ Other networks
Evaluation:	
Specialties	
☐ Products	☐ Markets serviced
☐ Services	

Fig. 7.1   Evaluation Checklist (Cont'd)

Company image

☐ Newspaper

☐ advertising Signs

☐ Radio, television

Evaluation:

☐ Office Internet

☐ Social media

☐ Other

Agents

☐ Professional demeanor

☐ Sales skills

☐ Team cooperation

Evaluate: How your background, style, people you know fit the profile of this company:

Other affiliated businesses

☐ Title companies/Escrow companies/Mortgage companies/Attorneys

Evaluation:

☐ Banks

☐ Builders

☐ Customers/clients

Summary

This chapter is important, for it gives you dozens of methods to figure out which company, office, and manager is right for you. Recommendations in this chapter:

- Research your choices carefully.

- Use the evaluation checklist in this chapter to assure you're covering all the bases. Going through these steps will not only help you make the right choice for you, but will give you information to hit the ground running!

Big Ideas from Chapter 7

- The company affiliations can be important, but they are much *less* important than the suitability of a particular office, manager, and the agents there.
- Gathering information from many sources within and outside of the business makes choosing the right office much easier.
- Separate the sales presentation from the real values and differences you see between companies and offices.
- Taking time to match a company's vision with your own professional vision and values ensures that you will get the right advantages as you start your career.

Get a Jump-Start on Success

- Gather your research about real estate companies by checking out the Web, affiliates, agents, and consumers.
- Attend brokers' opens and public open houses. Observe the agent's actions and the properties marketed by that firm.
- Contact three affiliates (a mortgage person, a title person—if you have title insurance in your area—and an escrow person) and find out the basics of their businesses as it pertains to working with them

CHAPTER 8

Getting Paid

"Get a spreadsheet comparison from your interviewer to compare the broker's fee structure based on various incomes. It may surprise you that royalties or transaction fees really start adding up as you complete more transactions."

~Chris Cross

In This Chapter

- How and When You Will Get Paid
- Company Compensation Models
- Gross isn't Net: What Comes Out of your Paycheck
- Additional Streams of Income for You
- Four Critical Questions to Ask about Compensation
- Big Ideas
- Get a Jump-Start to Success

You are almost ready to make those interview appointments. First, though, let me arm you with information about the various commission splits and payment plans evolving today. I say 'evolving', because new compensation plans are popping up daily—or at least, it seems like it. After exploring various commission structures, you will see four questions to ask in the interview to get the important information on each company's compensation plans.

When You Will Get Paid

Agents earn a commission when they sell a home, or when a home they have listed is sold by them or another agent. Listing a home for sale means that the agent signs some type of agreement with a homeowner. (There are several types of listing agreements, which you will learn about in pre-license school). The agent, referred to as a listing agent, markets the property to other agents, and to the public.

In the most common type of listing agreement, the exclusive listing agreement, the seller promises to pay a commission to the listing agency when a buyer purchases the property. If the listing company also *sells* the property, the company receives the whole commission, and distributes part of it to the agent or agents who listed and sold the property. If another company sells the property, part of the commission is paid to the selling agency (Fig. 8.1).

When Are Commissions Paid? Agents are paid only when buyers and sellers finalize the sale on a property (termed closing). This means that all paperwork regarding the transaction has been completed, and the monetary proceeds are available to the seller. Closing takes about one to two months from the date the offer to purchase is signed and accepted by the seller.

Agents are paid only for closings of properties listed, not for listing them. And not all properties listed sell. In one study, of all the homes listed in an area, less than half the properties listed during a half-year

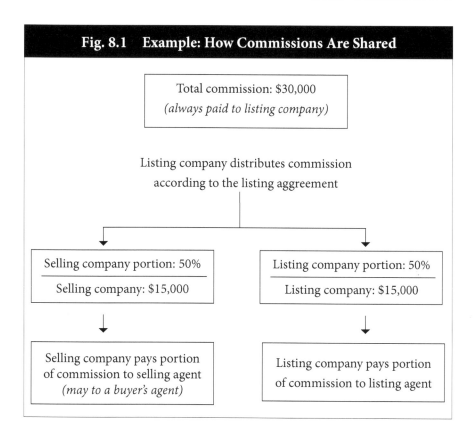

Fig. 8.1   Example: How Commissions Are Shared

Total commission: $30,000
(always paid to listing company)

Listing company distributes commission
according to the listing aggreement

Selling company portion: 50%

Selling company: $15,000

Listing company portion: 50%

Listing company: $15,000

Selling company pays portion
of commission to selling agent
(may to a buyer's agent)

Listing company pays portion
of commission to listing agent

period actually sold. Check your area and price range of listings sold in a normal time frame (your interviewer can tell you this).

How Much Is a Sale Worth? Commissions are generally based on the sale price of the property. Less commonly used methods to collect sales fees are as follows:

- A flat fee paid by the seller (sometimes charged wholly or partially regardless of whether the home is sold).
- Fees paid on a "menu" basis, that is, fees paid only on services actually provided. (This has been touted as a trend but has not gained much traction.)

- A commission based on listed price or sales price and paid by the *buyer*.
- A flat fee agreed to and paid by the buyer. The buyer usually has signed a "buyer-agency agreement" where the buyer agrees to pay a fee for the agent's services.

Each company and/or agent sets its rate of commission, and fees vary depending on the services the company and/or the agent provides. An example: A company pays a 6% commission. The total commission on closing of a $500,000 home is $30,000. This commission is divided between the companies involved in the transaction. Each company, in turn, pays the agent according to the contract the agent signed with the company.

Commission Splits and Company Services

Almost 90% of all real estate salespeople are paid exclusively through the commissions they earn. Here are the most common ways commissions are shared. The most recent NAR survey showed that 37% of REALTORS® were compensated under a fixed commission split (less than 100 percent), 23% with a graduated commission split (increases with productivity), and 15% with a capped commission split (rises to 100 percent after a predetermined threshold). Only 1% were salaried.

To receive a commission, agents must be licensed in that state and be affiliated with a licensed real estate company. All commissions due are paid to the *company*, and the company distributes the agent's portion to the agent. That portion varies from company to company.

The Funded Office: Commissions Paid on a Sliding Scale

We can divide commission schedules into two types: Funded and Fee. Funded means the agent pays the company from commissions earned. Fee means the agent pays a monthly desk fee.

The Funded Office. At the beginning of the year (either a calendar year or the agent's hiring anniversary, the "start-over" date), the agent splits the total commission dollars earned pretty evenly (such as 50/50) between the agent and the company. (Some companies start at 70/30, and the agent pays more of the operating expenses since he/she is getting more of the initial commission dollar). The year progresses and the agent is paid commissions.

At the same time, part of the gross commissions earned is going to the company to pay the company's operating expenses. (On a 50/50 split, 50 percent is going to the company). When the agent has paid the company a predetermined amount (ranging widely from about $15,000 to $35,000+), the agent reaches certain paid "commission plateaus." After the agent reaches a plateau, the agent is paid an increasingly greater proportion of the total commission.

Example: The agent starts at a 50/50 split. After the agent has paid the company the amount agreed to (through commissions), the agent gets more of the gross commission, say 60 percent, to the company's 40 percent. In some companies, the agent can reach a 100 percent plateau. In that scenario, after the agent has paid the required company dollar, the agent keeps *all* of the commission dollars until the agent reaches his start-over date (called the "anniversary date," usually the date the agent affiliated with the company).

Companies typically have two or three graduations in their commission plan, and these plateaus vary. Some companies have many plans available to their agents.

"Fee" Offices or a "Desk Fee"

The *total* commission paid to the company on a sale or listing is passed through the company to the agent (minus some fees like errors and omissions insurance). This desk fee allows the company to cover its expenses (and hopefully makes a profit so it stays in business). Desk fees range from approximately $400 to $2,000 or more per month. On the low end, this fee merely pays for the costs of being affiliated with a particular office. The owner has figured out the cost of running that office, and figures how much he or she should charge to "hang another license" on the wall. Most offices with low "desk fees" do not actually provide a desk.

Fig 8.2   Typical Graduated Commission Schedule

First Plateau of $20,000

"50/50" to $20,000 means the agent and company equally divide commissions earned by agent's sales/listings sold - figured on closed transactions only.

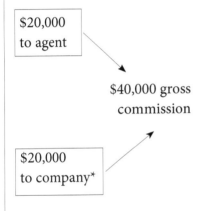

$20,000 to agent

$40,000 gross commission

$20,000 to company*

Second Plateau

"70/30" to $20,000 means after $20,000 has been paid to the company through transactions completed by the agent (sales/listings sold), the agent then receives 70% of the next gross commissions coming to the company as a result of agent's sales/listings sold (closed only).

50/50 commission split

70% of gross to commission agent

70/30 commission split

30% of gross to company

After the agent reaches a plateau, some companies award 100% of the commission dollars to the agent until the agent's next anniversary date.

*Company must be paid $20,000 to "trigger" the next plateau.

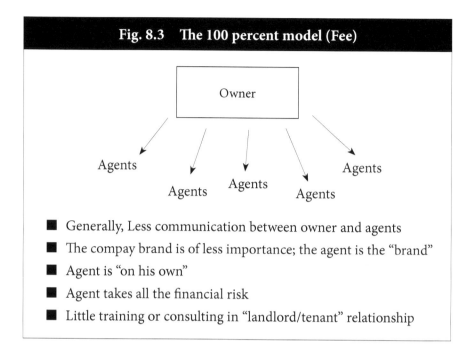

Fig. 8.3   The 100 percent model (Fee)

Owner

Agents   Agents

Agents   Agents   Agents

Agents

- Generally, Less communication between owner and agents
- The compay brand is of less importance; the agent is the "brand"
- Agent is "on his own"
- Agent takes all the financial risk
- Little training or consulting in "landlord/tenant" relationship

On the high end are offices that provide elaborate decor, mechanical and technical support (the latest in computers, etc.), support staff, and marketing materials. Paying a desk fee obligates the agent to budget carefully. Whether the agent sells a home that month or not, the agent owes that desk fee! (and will pay a hefty late fee if the fee is not paid on time).

 Find out the charges for late fees if you're considering a desk fee company.

The agent has the benefit of the company "umbrella," which may include institutional advertising and marketing pieces. Because all expenses are borne by the agent, many managers in the "fee" type of office do not hire new agents.

Find out the average costs of doing business in that office.

Since going it alone takes time, expertise, and more of the agent's own marketing money, it is estimated that desk fee agents actually retain about 65 percent of their gross dollars—a ratio comparable to traditional, or funded offices.

New Agents Probably Do Not Start at 100% in Fee Offices. Today, many 100% companies do not allow the new agent to start at 100 percent because they offer additional training and coaching services. These companies have learned that new agents need a high level of support to succeed. From an organizational standpoint, these companies are acting more like the traditional funded model, while keeping their independent instincts.

Companies Back Off the 100% Concept: The latest development in the 100% concept companies is that they—aren't. Now, the largest traditionally 100% company is requiring its agents to pay at least five percent to the company. Why? As company operating costs and agent demands have escalated, 100% companies have found it difficult to operate through merely collecting desk fees.

This trend toward split fees, rather than desk fees, has been building for years, because:

- Not enough agents can continue to pay those fees through the lean times.
- Agents are discovering that they really are not keeping 100 percent

Other Payment Plans

Client Fee-Based: Some companies have a menu of services that are offered to sellers or buyers. Agents in these companies receive a portion of the fees paid by the consumer. For example, rather than pay for the service, sellers may choose to show their own homes. They pay fees to the listing company for listing with the Multiple Listing Service (MLS) and fees for various advertising services.

Salaried: Although not common in residential real estate, a few companies offer salaries, or base plus commission. Look for variations of these payment plans in the next decade, as the complexities of representation create new opportunities for real estate specialists. In a few companies, bonuses are added for performance.

Don't Plan on Keeping it All!

There can be many debits from your commission check. They can include copy fees, coffee fees, errors and omissions insurance, parking, and marketing fees. Interestingly, many agents do not know how much is being deducted from their checks, or what the money is being paid for.

One company I interviewed charges only $400 per month to each associate to be affiliated with the company. This sounds too good to be true, and it is for those who intend to be productive. In addition to the $400 fee, this company charges $400 per transaction, plus various other fees. So, the more transactions one does with this company, the more it costs to be with them. Franchise fee payments can vary greatly too. One company tops out its fees each year when an agent has paid $3,000 to the company. Another franchise requires its agents to keep paying franchise fees for the entire year (This can amount to many thousands of dollars for a successful agent).

Companies tend to attract the kind of agents who match the payment structure. If you were affiliating with a company described earlier, would you likely be an agent who had high aspirations to complete many transactions in a year, or would you be the kind of agent who figures that you only are going to sell one home a quarter—so it is cheaper for you to be with a company like this?

How Companies Decide and Add Fees: In most companies, these fees are set by the company, and simply added to their agents' bills. The agents have no say in whether these fees will be charged or how much they will be. For example, one company tacked on a $10 per month "marketing fee." Another company attached a $25 transaction fee. Many agents today are concerned that they joined a company without realizing that these extra fees could escalate. In the last few years, these fees have gone from a few dollars per month per agent to quite a few hundred dollars a month per agent.

 Ask the manager for a 3-year historical review of additional fees. Ask how those fees are determined, and whether the agents have any say in if the fees will be charged. Ask what the average total of those fees is per month for the first-year agent, and for the experienced, successful agent.

In general, the more generous the commission to the agent, the fewer services, including training, coaching, and consulting support, are available. Also, in general, the less a company charges an agent in commission splits or desk fees, the higher the add-on charges.

Here's another "10" on the honesty scale. There's no free lunch. Invest money to build your career. What you pay should not be your biggest consideration in choosing a company. Here are your two biggest considerations:

- What you will keep (net, not gross).
- Your ability to earn and grow with that company (coaching, training, support, accountability, etc.).
- Other opportunities: Management, training, coaching, team building, expansion

What's Your Real Take Home Pay?

The generous commission structure you loved when you heard about it may not be the whole story. Ask the interviewer to put the various structures on a spreadsheet and compare the result of 4 transactions, 10 transactions, 15 transactions, and 20+ transactions. As you complete more transactions, the easy-peezy low-cost commission schedule that sounded so good may not be the best for you.

Note from reviewer Brian Leavitt: I've interviewed hundreds of candidates for my company. One of the first questions asked was, "How much do you charge?" That is the wrong question. The right question is, "How much can I make with you and how do I do that?" The truism: 100% of nothing is nothing.

Carla's note: From working with hundreds of real estate owners in all types of companies, I've found support for agent development is determined by the specific manager's interest in her agents. The commission splits tend to attract certain types of managers, but that varies greatly from office to office.

Other Ways to Get Paid: The Shared Revenue Model

The shared revenue model (Fig 8.4) emerged about 30 years ago, paralleling its introduction to business internationally. Here, the company shares additional revenues to commissions, which are usually paid in splits, just like the traditional "split revenue" company. These streams of income have various rules (how long an agent is with a company, how the money is earned, how the money is paid, if the stream can be sold or inherited, etc.)

Note: The attributes noted in figure 8.4 vary from company to company. This figure lists various attributes of shared revenue companies.

These additional revenues may include profit-sharing, stock options, or company-dollar revenues (what the company gets when an agent sells a home). Generally, these revenues are shared as a reward for helping the company grow. A Realtor® survey stated about 3% of all agents are in companies that provide the possibility of some kind of revenue sharing.

In one large franchise, agents refer another agent to the company to qualify to share profits. That way, the company grows, creating more revenue and profit, which are then shared.

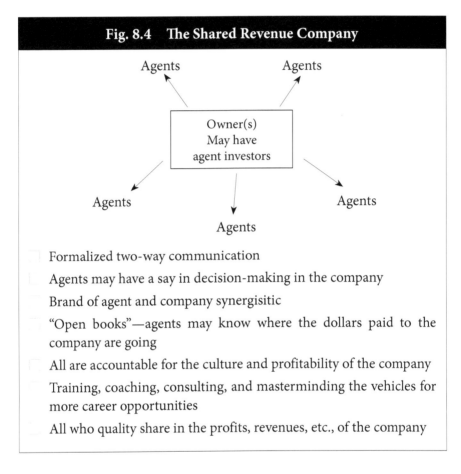

Fig. 8.4   The Shared Revenue Company

Formalized two-way communication

Agents may have a say in decision-making in the company

Brand of agent and company synergisitic

"Open books"—agents may know where the dollars paid to the company are going

All are accountable for the culture and profitability of the company

Training, coaching, consulting, and masterminding the vehicles for more career opportunities

All who quality share in the profits, revenues, etc., of the company

Now you have two lead-generating jobs if you want them: Finding leads for your business and finding recruits for your company. Find out exactly what those revenues are and how you can earn them before you commit to a shared revenue company. Remember, you must start your business by generating your own leads. And, in some companies, only certain high-producing agents are offered stock options, signing bonuses, or special deals. Be aware that these offerings may change at any time.

Note: These additional revenue streams you can earn are always voluntary. You don't' have to take part in the activities if you don't want to earn additional revenue streams..

Choose the Type of Company You Want to Fit Your Career Goals

Too often, agents choose a company based on the perceived attractiveness of the commission splits. That's like choosing to buy a stripped-down model of a car—and then finding out you're going to have to add thousands of dollars to it to make it the kind of car you want to drive.

The difference in what you pay one company or another may be small when you compare the leverage you receive through effective training, coaching, and consulting to catapult your career forward.

Look at choosing your real estate company as you would choose your graduate school in college. Which will launch you into the best career the fastest?

Which will challenge you? Which has the best opportunities for your career advancement?

Big Ideas from Chapter 8

- Comparing compensation plans can be daunting.
- Services vary greatly with each company.
- Add-on costs can completely change the amount of commission dollars you actually bring home. Focus on net, not gross.
- Other streams of income may be available. These can be confusing, too. Get in writing exactly what these are and what you must do to obtain them.
- Pricing reflects a company's values.
- What does the pricing structure really say about the company? Is that image the same as the interviewer is conveying?

Get a Jump-Start on Success

Ask these four questions about compensation during the interview. After the interview, write your pros and cons for each of the answers you receive.

1. What are your compensation plans? Get in writing each plan and the consequences of each part of the plan. Get a list of the services provided in writing.

2. What are the costs that come out of my paycheck? What do they do for me? Get a list of these costs and how they accrue. Especially focus on franchise fees. Do they top out, or go on until your anniversary year starts again?

3. Explain these other streams of income. Who is eligible? How does one qualify? How does the operation work? Is the stream forever? How often is the plan changed, and who can change the plan? Get the plan in writing. Get an example—preferably a first-year agent and his/her earnings from this additional stream of income.

4. Given your pricing structure, how do you help agents grow within their businesses?

CHAPTER 9

How to Get the Most from Your Interview

"In the interview process, an agent should ask what a manager's standards of practice are. For example: Do they hire part-time agents? Do they hire people who won't attend and do the work during the training program? Be aware of the difference between a persuasive sales spiel and honesty."

~ Cindy Zulla, manager and trainer

In This Chapter:

- Your Time Frame for Interviewing
- How to Prepare for the Interview
- The Day of the Interview
- Five Critical Questions to Ask your Interviewer
- Evaluate the Interview and the Manager
- Three Qualities Important in a Manager
- What to Expect in the Second Interview
- Big Ideas
- Get a Jump-Start to Success

If you are new to the profession, you are getting closer to the reality of real estate sales. Your next step will be to interview for a sales position. If you are experienced, but thinking about a change in company or office, you need this chapter as well. When things are going wrong, an agent may think merely changing companies will do the trick. Then, she chooses a company that promises almost magically to solve the agent's problems. It is not that simple.

Real estate sales practices vary widely from city-to-city, street-to-street, and from agent-to-agent. You will see this in the interviews. Some interviewers will ask you to participate in two-to-four-part interviews. Some will attempt to hire you after a five-minute chat. (I hope you doubt that hiring you after a few minutes means you are special.) Here are tips to manage the interview process to get all the information you need to make the right decision.

Your Time Frame for Interviewing

The complete interview process can take from a single one-hour session to several interviewers over several weeks. Fig. 9.1 shows you the flow and time frame for a typical interview process.

Who Interviews You? You may be scheduled with a recruiter, a coach, assistant manager, or manager. It depends on how the company and office is structured. In large offices, the first interview for new agents is usually done by a coach or assistant manager. In this book, I will refer to all interviewers as "managers".

When Will You be Scheduled? Most managers do not interview new agents until the interviewee is scheduled for his or her license exam or has passed the exam. In general, start interviewing seriously about three weeks before you are scheduled to take your exam. Why? You will want time to schedule:

- Initial appointments with the three to five offices you have chosen
- Second appointments with those offices
- Fact-gathering about those offices

Fig. 9.1   The Interview Process

1. **Make appointment for the first interview:**
   - ❐ Take your résumé—even if the interviewer doesn't ask for it
   - ❐ Prepare question to ask
   - ❐ Bring a notebook to record answers
   - ❐ Manager may ask you to complete an application
     (That's a good sign. After all, real businesses do that, don't they?)

2. **First interview, approximately 1 hour:**
   - ❐ Manager asks questions to qualify you
   - ❐ Agent gathers information, asks questions
   - ❐ Manager makes appointment for second interview
     (If mutually agreeable.)

   Our recommendation: Request a second interview. Don't let yourself be hired at the first interview.

3. **After the first interview:**
   - ❐ Evaluate manager's interview process, organizational skills, materials used
   - ❐ If manager thinks you aren't a match for that office, manager won't set a second interview

4. **Second interview, approximately 1 hour:**
   - ❐ Interviewer/manager exchange questions/information
   - ❐ Manager asks for affiliation, or
   - ❐ Manager asks for more information
     (Visit your home, meet spouse, or further interview.)

5. **Decision**

After the first interview:

- Evaluate the interviewer's process, organizational skills, and materials used.

- If the interviewer thinks you are not a match for that office, the interviewer will not set a second interview.

- Note: You may be referred to another interviewer, perhaps the manager, assistant manager, or coach

Second interview, approximately 1 hour:

- Interviewer/manager exchange questions/information. Interviewer asks for affiliation or asks for more information (visit your home, meet spouse, or further interview).

Making the Decision

As you choose a particular office, follow the process suggested here. Too often, an interviewee gets excited about a sales pitch and is flattered at being offered a position quickly. (You may be offered a position so quickly your head will spin…) Also, pay close attention to how the interview is constructed. *Sales presentations should not come first.* If that is all you hear, you may be flattered and quickly join an office before gathering enough information to make the best choice, and you will later find out you didn't get the whole story.

Next to your decision to make real estate your career, choosing your manager and office, in that order, are the most important decisions you will make. These choices will be a major determinant to how quickly you are successful.

Arrange for the Interview

Call the managers of the offices in which you are interested. Ask for an appointment. Ask who will be doing the initial interview. This may be a recruiter, a manager, an assistant manager, or a coach. This initial interview will usually be 45 to 90 minutes. When you make the appointment, ask:

- If you should send any materials before the interview.

- If you should fill out an application in advance. (See figure 9.2 for items on an application)

- Which materials, if any, you should supply prior to the interview, or bring to the interview.

Managers can do a much better interview when they have a chance to review the information on an application, identify areas of concern, and perceive the strengths of the interviewee. This information helps managers zero in on important areas of discussion, saving time for the candidate and the manager.

Phone or Online Screening Questions: To save time and prescreen applicants, managers or their assistants may ask preliminary questions over the phone or via online survey. Some common ones are:

- "Do you intend to work in real estate as your main source of income?"
- "Have you already passed your license exam?"

Compare these initial processes among the offices you choose. If you have interviewed for a position in a different field, or have ever been an interviewer, compare the professionalism of the process in these offices with the processes previously experienced. The real estate manager with a professional initial system will most likely carry that philosophy through other management practices.

One of the best and most successful owners I know has a four-part screening process. If you pass his criteria, you know you've been picked to be a part of a special, successful group. Predictably, that manager has a top-producing office with little turnover.

After the Call: Send a note (hand-written is best) to thank the interviewer for his or her time and say you are looking forward to the interview. Successful managers typically have five to ten interviews per week. The person who writes a note is always more impressive. Managers assume the interviewee will follow up with leads and clients just as attentive as with the manager.

Fig. 9.2   In a Real Estate Application

Personal information, *such as:*
- ❒ Name
- ❒ Address
- ❒ Phone/email

Real estate experience, *such as:*
- ❒ Licensing In another state
- ❒ Sales activity

General information, *such as:*
- ❒ Why real estate as a career
- ❒ Earnings expectations
- ❒ Why affiliate with this company

Work history, *such as:*
- ❒ Employer name, address
- ❒ Job description
- ❒ Income, reason for leaving

Education history, *such as:*
- ❒ Public school, years
- ❒ College, years
- ❒ Course of study

Personal references:
- ❒ Name, address
- ❒ Relationship, profession

Decide on Your Preferences

You are getting ready to go into the interview. Do you know what you are looking for? Use the checklist below, Exhibit 9.3, to decide what kind of company, office, and atmosphere you'll feel most comfortable in.

Fig. 9.3   Your Preferences

Selling vs. Non-Selling Manager
❏ You prefer a manager who doesn't sell real estate. (non-competing)
❏ You prefer a manager who sells real estate. (may provide a good role model/may be too busy to help you)

Training
❏ You prefer a formalized training program.
❏ You prefer to "go it on your own", with the manager avaliable to answer questions.

Large vs. Small Office
❏ You prefer a large, busy office.
❏ You prefer a small, more laid-back atmosphere.

Large vs. Small Company
❏ You like the idea of a large company behind your efforts.
❏ You like the idea of a boutique, specialist company.

Many vs. Few New Agents
❏ You want to be around other new agents like you, so you prefer an office with lots of new agents.
❏ You want to be with seasoned agents and would rather be among the few new agents in the office.

Top Producer Assignment
❏ You want to be assigned to a top producer to find out how that top producer works and perhaps do work for that top producer.
❏ You want to become an above-average producer fast and don't want to be in the shadows of anyone else.

Age of Agents
❏ You want to be around people your age.
❏ You want ro be around people of a wide range of ages and interests.

Work from Office vs. Work from Home
❏ You want to work from the office and have a desk at the office.
❏ You want to work from home.

No Supervision/Management
❏ You prefer little or on supervision. You'll go at your own speed.
❏ You want and expect leadership and guidance as you start your career.

Coach vs. No Coach
❏ You want a coach dedicated to your success.
❏ You prefer to go it alone and operate independently.

Mentor vs. Manager
❏ You want a mentor - someone you can go to ask questions any time.
❏ You want to go to your manager as your trusted adviser.

Team vs. No Team
❏ You are considering working with a team.
❏ You want to work on your own.
❏ You like a team atmosphere. You want to be able to go to anyone and get support.
❏ You prefer a "go it alone" atmosphere.

Prepare for the Interview

Clothing: As you interview other agents as you visit their open houses, note how they are dressed. Do they look as though they are ready and qualified to help clients spend hundreds of thousands of dollars? Or, do they look as though real estate is something they fit in between recreational pursuits?

Even if you find that the salespeople in your area and your desired office dress casually, you should dress for your interview in a conservative, businesslike manner. That means:

- For men, a conservative shirt, jacket, and tie (unless you are in a casual market area, and you have observed that no one, including the owner of the company, ever wears ties and jackets). Clothes are clean; shirt is ironed; sleeves on jacket are appropriate, and shoes are shined. Briefcase is polished and organized.

- For women, a business dress, a conservative suit or skirt and jacket. No exceedingly short skirts, low necklines, flashy jewelry, heavy makeup, eye-catching hose, or evening shoes. Clothes are clean and ironed; shoes are shined. Purse and/or briefcase are polished and organized.

- Well-groomed hair, nails, of course.

- Accessories are clean and polished (briefcases/purses, etc.)

Be Conservative. Why? Because clients judge you in the first few seconds. They ask themselves whether they believe you are the type of person to whom they can entrust their money. As you interview, pretend the manager is your customer, which is true because you are selling yourself.

One of the biggest concerns managers grapple with is, "How can I tactfully teach my agents to dress more appropriately for the office?" The best way to solve that sensitive problem is to hire agents who already understand the importance of conservative, appropriate business dress. The more the manager perceives you as a problem, the less he or she will want to hire you.

Your Car: Be sure your car is clean—outside and inside. Observant managers find out what car you drive, and its condition. I will never forget the day I got into an agent's car to inspect a property. I hadn't seen

Remove all barriers to getting hired!

her car before (not smart). That car looked like a little garbage dump and it was *old* garbage. It struck me like a bolt of lightning: That car absolutely represented our company image (and hers) to the buyer who got into it (and probably got into it only once).

What to Take to the Interview. Bring along your résumé or application, even if you sent them before the interview. Managers have been known to lose résumés and applications. If you bring a résumé, be sure your résumé specifically addresses real estate sales. When I read résumés that are general, I think the interviewee is shopping for an occupation. Your résumé should be short, concise, and easy-to-read. If you are unsure about how to write your résumé, check out one of the many excellent books and online resources available on how to create an effective résumé.

 Managers are looking for the traits they think are important—not for a list of credentials. This chapter will show you the qualities and the behaviors managers value.

Complete Any Manager-Given Assignments—Shows Positive Sales Traits. Be sure to do *all* assignments the manager has given you, such as completing the application. Providing your information prior to the interview allows managers to prepare. When the candidate shows up with application in hand, or an incomplete application, managers conclude that the candidate is not too interested.

From my tone, you can probably guess that one of the qualities I want to see demonstrated by the applicant's behavior is *accountability*. I use the application process to see whether the interviewee *comes through* on his promise to complete and provide me the paperwork before the interview. If not, will he carry through on promises to a client? Another attribute I look for is *willing to learn from his leader*. If you are not willing to reflect the team values now, what will happen when you join?

Your Goals for the Interview. You have two objectives:

- Gather information.
- Sell yourself.

Manager's Goals for the Interviews. The manager also has two objectives:

- Gather information.
- Sell the company, office, and himself.

Who Asks Questions First? Both you and the manager have the same objectives, to gather information and to sell yourselves. Good managers take control of the interview by asking questions to qualify the candidate. Their objective is to see if the candidate's background, skills, and traits match the job description they have developed for successful agents. Then, after finding out whether that agent is a match, they answer questions and sell the interviewee on the benefits of joining the office. They demonstrate professional sales techniques.

Qualify First. Would you put a client in your car before you found out they could buy and that they were the kind of person you wanted to work with? I hope you wouldn't, but many agents fail to qualify potential clients and waste time—both theirs and the clients.

Fig.9.4 shows the agent's process in qualifying, showing, and closing clients. It is the same process managers use to interview agents.

Fig. 9.4 The Sales Process		
Agent/buyer sales process		**Manager/interview process**
1. Agent qualifies buyer.	QUALIFY ➤	Manager qualifies agent.
2. Agent shows homes.	SELL BENEFITS ➤	Manager shows benefits (to customer agent) of joining office.
3. Agent closes buyer.	CLOSE ➤	Manager closes agent.

The Day of the Interview

Arrive ten minutes early. Before you go into the manager's office, note:

Exterior of Office—Maintenance: What does that say about the image of the office/company?

Demeanor of the Receptionist and Other Support Staff: Are they friendly, attentive, and courteous?

Note from reviewer Brian Leavitt, as he interviewed for his company: "My receptionist gave me feedback on the candidate's behavior. If the candidate was rude to my support staff, I drew the conclusion that this candidate would not fit into our culture".

Interior of Office: Is it clean and neat? Pretend you are a potential client. Are you made comfortable? Would you be proud to have your clients come in?

Atmosphere of Office: Are agents relaxing in the reception area? (This is not a good sign!) Is the office humming with activity? (This will vary greatly office-to-office, also depending on whether the agents have offices offsite)

Office Portfolio: Is there information about the office and the company available in the lobby? There may be a hard copy, or a story being told on a screen.

The Interview Room. Is it apparent that the interviewer is ready for you? Is the interview room set up for an interview?

The Interview. Let the interviewer lead the way.

How *not* to Start the Interview

OK. These are my pet peeves. The candidate sits down and immediately:

- Tries to take over the interview
- Asks about commission splits
- Quickly tells me she wants a special commission arrangement or other benefits
- Ask what I'm going to do for her (because she's so exceptional...)
- Tells me which other companies have already offered her a position

Starting with this tone and these statements or questions is getting off onto the wrong foot. These are immediate turn-offs and it is difficult for me even to continue the interview! I want to feel this prospective agent will let me be the leader, the educator, and the coach.

Another "10" on the honesty scale: If the manager lets you take over from the get-go, then they are not skilled interviewers, or just focused on selling you without knowing who you are.

What the Manager Is Looking For

Good interviewers ask you specific, planned questions to discover:

- If you have the traits and qualities of a successful agent in that office
- If you have a sales behavioral profile

- If you are motivated to succeed in sales
- The skills you bring to the business, such as sales, management and computer skills
- If you have shared values with the office and will be a positive addition to the culture and team

Look back at figure 1.3 to see my list of successful salesperson qualities.

The Questions Best Interviewers Ask. Fig. 9.5 lists some behavioral-based questions with the traits and qualities that they indicate. They are termed behavioral-based questions because they ask the interviewee to recall his *past behavior.* Behavioral-based questions give us the best indicators of a person's relative strengths of character, and how they will apply these strengths in sales.

Why are behavioral-based questions so important to the interview process? Because *behavior that's rewarded is repeated.*

Fig. 9.5   Behavioral-Based Questions and What They Tell Us

Describe a situation in your life where you failed miserably. Everyone told you that you should never attempt that again. How did you handle that failure? And what did you do next?

Answer indicates relative tenacity and mental toughness, belief in oneself.

Describe a time in your life when you took a risk. What happened?

Answer indicates amount of personal initiative.

Describe a time in your life when you went to get a job. How did you go about it?

Answer indicated ability to make sales calls, sell yourself, and self-start your career.

Your Turn: Get Information

After the initial questioning period, led by the manager, it is your turn to ask questions.

The Five Critical Questions to Ask—for Sure

Here are the critical questions to ask, with some tips in how to judge the answers.

What are your minimum production expectations for agents in their first 3 months? 6 months? 1 year? This question will tell you whether you are considering joining an office of focused, career-minded professionals, or an office of part-timers, low producers, and those who just want to snag a couple of sales. If the manager has no minimum expectations, he/she is willing to hire anyone to "give them a chance." That is not a business. It is an opportunity to create an avocation. Low expectations also mean there will not be a given, coached, business start-up plan, since any action (or lack of action) is okay.

How are you going to help me launch my career? Describe your start-up program and schedule for me—onboarding, training, and business

Fig. 9.6   The Five Critical Questions to Ask—for Sure
1. What are your minimum production expectations for agents in their first 3 months? 6 months? 1 year?
2. How are you going to help me launch my career?
3. What kind of results does your start-up plan and initial training gain for your new agents? How many transactions are they doing, on average, by month 3?
4. Coaching and Accountability: Do you use a start-up plan? Who will be coaching me to the start-up plan? How will I be held accountable?
5. What other specific support will assure I will be successful fast?

start-up plan. Ask to see the programs themselves. Every interviewer will tell you they have an awesome training program. That's why you want to see it. Are there objectives, curriculum, and teaching outline?

Onboarding. You would be amazed at how many real estate offices do not have an orientation resource or onboarding process for you. I do not mean, "We'll show you around the office and how to use the copy machine."

Without these systems and processes, new agents have no way to find out where the files are, how to get the various keys, codes, and operations associated with the office, the Multiple Listing Services, and the National Association of REALTORS® information. Lack of these checklists and systems indicates that the manager either does not care much about the quick success of the new agent, or that he/she does not hire many new agents.

Schedule: Ask for a timeline and schedule of the whole process this office will use to help you develop your career. This will show you whether there is a comprehensive plan, or just a haphazard series of events.

What kind of results does your start-up plan and initial training gain for your new agents? How many transactions are they doing, on average, by month 3? Ask to see the statistics.

Great. There's a top producer in the office. That may have little to do with your own success. Sadly, some offices 'feed' top producing agents to help them keep their status. There seems to be one set of rules for everyone except those top producers. In those offices, second-tier agents start feeling they will never be able to crack the 'clique' or become one of the 'cool kids'. This atmosphere is not good for your growth potential!

Coaching and Accountability: Do you use a start-up plan? Who will be coaching me to the start-up plan? How will I be held accountable?
What will the coach use as a game plan? What is the cost? Is the coach *trained* as a coach? What support, training, and monitoring do the *coaches* have? Talk to a newer agent in that office who has been coached. If there is no formal, scheduled coaching, and no or little accountability, you're on your own to figure it out.

What other specific support will assure I will be successful fast?
Listen carefully to this answer. Is it a "branding speech" to sell you the benefits of that company, or does it focus on helping you individually reach your goals? If the interviewer mentions support services, such as peer coaching, delve deeper to find out what specific services they provide.

What Your Success Is NOT About: I wish I could tell you that your success will be related to the company's image in the market. However, it is much more related to the way your career will be developed (business start-up-plan, coaching, and training). I have seen so many agents fail in "great" companies because they did not have a start-up plan, a great training program, or a trained coach. They wandered around in indecision until their money ran out.

More Questions, Topics, and Areas to Explore

Based on the answers you gave in figure 9.1, check the areas below you want to explore in the interview (figure 9.7)

Getting Me Started in the Office

How will you get me started fast? What is your overall program?

(Ask to see the specific structure of the program.)

What is your orientation/onboarding process?

(Ask to see the specific packets and an outline of the process, so you know it's for real.) You don't want to be wandering around trying to figure out the basics three months from now.

Do you have the operations of the office systematized?

(Ask to see the operations/systems so you know how in-depth it really is.)

Do you have a business start-up plan for me?

Fig. 9.7   Interview topics and questions

The Office

❏ What is your vision for your office? Your mission? (Ask to see them)

❏ What do agents specialize in here?

❏ What geographical areas does the office serve?

❏ What is your agent turnover rate?

❏ Will l get an assigned desk? If there a fee for an assigned desk?

❏ What it your average price range?

❏ What is your client profile?

❏ Are there teams in the office organized by a "rainmaker" (lead agent)? Describe them.

❏ Is there teamwork in the office? Please describe.

❏ How many transactions, on average, do new agents complete here in their first year?

Agent Profiles

❏ How many agents are in the office now? What are your recruiting goals for this year? How many do you want to hire this year?

❏ How many are less than a year in the business?

❏ How many are part-timers?

❏ What are the average number of sales per agent? Listings per agent?

In-Office Support

❏ What is your availability? Would you show me your schedule/calendar?

❏ Do you have an assistant manager? What is his/her job description?

❏ Describe your office staff. How will they assist me?

❏ Show me the resources in the office. (Library, computers, etc.)

Support for Productivity

❏ Show me the systems and materials you have to help me promote myself. How do you distribute referrals that come into the office?

❏ Is there a fee for them?

Fig. 9.7   Interview topics and questions (cont'd)

❑ Describe your advertising policies and fees.

❑ Do you schedule floor time? How?

❑ Do you encourage agents to hold open houses? Why or why not?

Management

❑ Please describe your background, education, training, designations, and strengths.

❑ Describe how you commununicate with agents.

❑ Do you sell? What percent of your time is spent selling?

❑ Do you hire all those who interview with you? If not, how do you make your hiring choices?

❑ Describe your management style. What is important to you?

❑ Where do you see real estate in 3 years? 10 years?

❑ How do you get new information?

❑ How do you communicate it?

❑ What are you doing differently this year? Why?

Company Profile

❑ What is the company best at? (Marketing, training, sales, etc., - companies should have one core competency that they can name easily.)

❑ What is exceptional about this company?

❑ What are its challenges today?

❑ Show me the company vision and mission.

❑ Is it is Realtor® company?

❑ How much as the company grown in the past year? Past 5 years?

❑ Describe its growth goals for the year. Next 3 years.

Marketing Strategies

❑ How does the company advertise itself?

❑ What community service strategies does the company take part in?

❑ Explain your marketing strategies as a company and the philosophy behind them.

Fig. 9.7   Interview topics and questions (cont'd)

Services Provided and Fees

❒ Describe the errors and commissions insurance coverage.

❒ Do we have access to a company attorney?

❒ How are our calls answered during weekdays and weekends?

❒ What phone number is on our signs? (the agent's or the company's?)

❒ Does the company have health, dental or retirement plans available?

❒ Please provide me with a list of all costs associated with becoming an agent with you.

Commission Schedules

❒ Describe your commission schedules and the philosophy behind them.

❒ Do you make some exceptions to your commission schedule - and, if so why?

❒ What is the most important service and value I'll be getting from you?

Mutual Expectations and Standards*

❒ What are your production standards for a new agent for his/her 3 months? 6 months? First year?

❒ How do you assist new agents in reaching and exceeding these standards?

❒ If you don't have standards, why not?

❒ What are my consequences if I don't meet those standards?

❒ What are the production standards of experienced agents?

❒ Are there agents here who aren't reaching standards*? How many?

❒ What are the consequences if an experienced agent does not meet standards?

❒ Do you have a program to help experienced agents meet and exceed standards?

Standards are not goals. They are minimum expectations.

(Ask to see it.) If you're told you will make your own plan, watch out. How would you know the priorities?

Will you provide me a coach? Fee? Game plan? Coaches' training?

(Ask to see the coaches' training outline, so you know it's a real coaching program.)

What will my schedule be for the first week? First month?

(Ask to see it.)

Can you provide your agent's job description?

(Ask to see it.)

What systems do you have to get agents started fast?

(Let me see them.)

How do you work with me to ensure my success?

(Let me see your coaching schedule.)

What are your success statistics? (Ask to see them.)

Remember, though, that the success of a few agents doesn't mean you will be successful.

Education/Training

How important do you think training is to an agent's success? What is your training program for me as a new agent or, as a transferring agent?

(Ask to see the topics and schedule for the training programs.)

What are the objectives of your new agent training program? What do you expect of me during the new agent training? What will I be able to do as a result?

How often is new agent training offered?

(Ask to see the course schedule, course descriptions, course syllabuses, and training calendar.)

Who trains? What are their qualifications?

Who wrote the program? Describe this person's background and expertise. Are your trainers professionally trained and auditioned?

Describe your training programs and consulting for experienced agents. How do you help experienced agents get to the next career level? (Courses, Masterminds, etc.)

Describe your technology training and support.

What technology will assist me as I start my career? Is there training for that technology? What is the cost of the tech use and/or the training? Is there someone in the office I can go to with tech questions?

Provide statistics of new people and when they made their first sale. How is your program different and better from others?

The Office

What's your vision for your office? Your mission?

(Ask to see them.)

What do agents specialize in here?

What geographical areas does the office serve? What's your agent turnover rate?

Explain how desks/no desks work here.

What is your average price range? What's your client profile?

Are there teams in the office organized by a "rainmaker" (lead agent)? Describe them.

Is there teamwork in the office? Please describe.

How many transactions, on average, do new agents complete here in their first year?

Agent Profiles

How many agents are in the office now? What are your recruiting goals for this year? How many do you want to hire this year?

How many are less-than-a-year in the business? How many are part-timers?

What is the average number of sales per agent? Listings per agent?

In-Office Support

What's your availability? Would you show me your schedule/calendar? Do you have an assistant manager? What's his/her job description?

Describe your office staff. How will they assist me?

Show me the resources in the office? (Library, computers, etc.)

Support for Productivity

Show me the systems and materials you have to help me promote myself. How do you distribute referrals that come into the office?

Is there a fee for them?

Describe your advertising policies and fees.

Do you encourage agents to hold open houses? Why or why not?

Describe how the technology developed by the company (or recommended by the company) will assist me to develop my business.

Management

Please describe your background, education, training, designations, and strengths.

Describe how you communicate with agents.

Do you sell? What percent of your time is spent selling?

Do you hire everyone who interviews with you? If not, how do you make your hiring choices?

Describe your management style.

Where do you see real estate in three years? Ten years?

How do you get new information? How do you communicate it?

What are you doing differently this year? Why?

Company Profile

What is the company best at? (Marketing, training, sales, etc.—companies should have one core competency that they can name easily.)

What's exceptional about this company/office?

What are its challenges today?

Show me the company vision and mission. Is it a Realtor® company?

How much has the company grown in the past year? Past five years? Describe its growth goals for the year. Next three years.

Marketing Strategies

How does the company advertise itself?

What community service strategies does the company take part in? Explain your marketing strategies as a company and the philosophy behind them.

Services Provided and Fees

Describe the errors and omissions insurance coverage. Do we have access to a company attorney?

Does the company have health, dental, or retirement plans available?

Please provide me with a list of all costs associated with becoming an agent, a Realtor®, an agent with you.

Commission Schedules

Describe your commission schedules and the philosophy behind them.

Do you make some exceptions to your commission schedule—and, if so, why? What is the most important service and value I'll be getting from you?

Bottom line: What is in It for Me? Find out the "what," the "how," and the "why it will benefit me" of every program mentioned by the manager. Do not be afraid to ask probing questions about a program you do not understand. In fact, the biggest mistake interviewees make is not asking for a clarification and visual of a particular program.

Did You Take a Behavioral Profile?

There is a trend in the real estate industry to become more systematic about interviewing to avoid hiring mistakes. Behavioral profiles are becoming more commonly used early in the interview process. The behavioral profile shows us the preferred behavioral style of an individual. Note: The results of these profiles cannot be used to hire or not. They are merely one of the tools to help candidates understand their own profiles. The behavioral profile is used to validate the behaviors managers are hearing about and observing in the interview.

For You as a New Agent: Taking a behavioral profile and having someone validate it with you is a huge benefit. It will give you indicators regarding your success, and whether you will LIKE selling real estate.

You've Made It Through the First Interview

Some managers attempt to "close" the interviewee at the end of the first interview. (Agents have told me they have been asked to join the office within the first fifteen minutes of an initial interview!) Be wary of any manager who attempts to hire you without thoroughly investigating your qualifications. This investigation, by the way, takes longer than fifteen minutes. After all, the manager should be matching a prospective agent to the job description and desired agent qualities for that office.

Unless you are comfortable with the manager and the office, express your interest and ask to get back together with the manager within the next few days. Why? Because you want to get enough information to be *sure* of your decision.

Look Around Before You Leave

At the end of this interview, ask to see the office. Note the work spaces, support services, and mechanical support, such as computers. Look at the layout of the office. Where would your desk be? Is it a "bullpen" configuration? Are desks shared? How are desk assignments determined? Does everyone work from home? You can find out a lot about management philosophy by analyzing the floor plan.

Meet some of the agents while you are touring the office. What is their attitude about another new person? Are they cordial? Some offices joke that they refuse to learn new agents' names for three months— because they probably will not be there that long! Do you think you will get help—or hindrance—from the associates?

Does the company structure support experienced agents in helping you succeed? Or not?

What to Do Between Interview Appointments

Between the first and second interviews you have lots of work to do. This is where you *really* get the true picture of that office, manager, and agents.

- Ask to attend an office meeting. That can really be revealing, and I think it's essential.

- Ask to go on an office tour of new listings if the office tours. Ride with some experienced agents, and ask them questions about the office, company, and manager. You may get a grumbler or two, but that is revealing too.

- Ask the manager for the names of two or three agents who have been with the office less than six months. Call them and ask, "How did you get started? What were the biggest challenges? How did the manager help you? If you could do something differently, what would it be?"

- Inspect the office inventory with the manager. Be sure to ask, "How did that agent get that listing?"

- Request a list of agents in that office and ask which ones you should talk to. Talk to those people, but also talk to others on the list—the more, the better. Ask the experienced agents about the office organization, culture, hiring philosophy, and their feelings about the office. Is there challenge and encouragement for professional growth?

- Interview with the owner of the company, if possible (if he or she is not also the manager). As the leader, that person sets the tone for the entire company. You need to feel that their vision is closely related to your career goals. Matching visions and values is much more important than the money or services offered by a company. Do you think there is something in it for that leader to help you get started? What would that be?

Evaluate the Interview and the Manager

You have completed the first interview. Now it is time to evaluate the interview *and* the manager. Why now? Because if you decide not to continue with this office, *now* is the time to stop it. Evaluate the manager's professionalism, skill, dedication, and organization in choosing the right candidates.

Manager's Professionalism: Did the interview request information from you prior to the interview?

Screening System: Were you asked questions on the phone or did you complete an online survey? Did you complete an application? A well-thought-out screening system indicates care in picking agents to work with. Such a manager will spend more time with each person hired, to assure each new agent of getting a great start toward a dynamic career.

Manager's Goal: From the way the manager approaches the interview, you can determine whether he or she actually has a job description for an agent and is attempting to match it to you. Or, is the manager just looking for another body to fill a desk—or another license on the wall?

Qualifying or Selling? In the sales process, qualifying the "buyer" always precedes selling the benefits of the product, service, or company. If the process is reversed, the salesperson can end up selling something to someone who may not want to buy it or may not be qualified to buy it. Let the manager take the lead. If the manager sells and does not do a thorough job of qualifying you for the position, you can conclude that the manager doesn't understand the sales process. Or, she doesn't care if the candidate is qualified. She just wants that license on the wall.

Quality of Questions: Do they force you to think? Do they launch you into the past? Do they seem to be focused on finding more about you and qualifying you? Or are they "future-based," giving you the opportunity to "shine it on," make up answers you think the interviewer will love, dream, and impress your interviewer? If the interviewer is skilled, he or she will ask you past-based (behavioral) questions almost exclusively.

Manager as Role Model: Did the manager exhibit sales organization, qualifying skills, and sales skills? Did he/she have physical evidence of his/her claims? How much were you asked to believe without proof?

Systematic Interview Process: Does the manager have a systematic interview procedure? Does the manager take notes, so he or she can remember what to delve into more deeply in the second interview? These are signs of professionalism and skill.

Manager Also Sells: More than 50 percent of all managers/owners today also *sell* real estate. Although they can be successful at both, be sure the selling manager sees himself in a true management role, and that he/she has the systems and organization to assure your successful start. Will she have time for you?

Reliance on Company Benefits: In my experience, less competent managers rely on company benefits to "sell" their candidates. ("Our company is first in technology," or, "We're the biggest… you'll be more successful here," or, "Our company has been in the area 50 years."). Strong, creative managers explain the benefits of that office.

Overall Impression—Looking for the Next Team Member, or Just Another Licensee: Managers are under pressure to keep adding licenses to their "wall." Is it your impression that is the case here? Or, is the manager carefully screening candidates to be sure they are positive additions to the team?

Three Qualities Great Managers Share

Ask for a job description for that manager. The description should include: "To find and develop each agent to his highest potential. To do that, I recruit with purpose, select carefully, coach and train to production, set and keep high standards, and lead to our vision and values."

Committed to Your Success—This means all those systems and organizations are in place to assure you have a smooth, successful start. Your manager needs to be committed to starting new agents in their careers—not just hiring them as an after-thought.

Attitude and Preparation—Enthusiastic and reasonably up to date with sales strategies and technology; this does not mean he is a techie, but that he stays up with the trends and is encouraging agents to try new things.

Thinks of Herself as a Trainer/Coach—You want a manager whose job it is to develop individual careers—not just create schedules, go to meetings, or handle crises. In other words, you need much more than an "answer man."

What Top Agents Say They Want in a Manager

To write this book, I surveyed dozens of top agents. Here are some of their comments about choosing the right manager:

- From Marie Farnsworth: "Look for a manager who is enthusiastic."

- From Tom Raynor: "Look for a manager who is a leader, who will be there for guidance when you need it."
- From Cindy Zulla: "The best manager is one who will act as your mentor or coach. Be willing to let your manager hold you accountable to your goals."
- From Connie Kruse: "An ideal atmosphere would be strong in knowledge, integrity and spirit. I researched companies to find a company that matched my values."
- From Raymond Megie: "Ask for references of other new agents who started in that office. Get their opinions. Surround yourself with people who are proactive."

What to Expect in the Second Interview

Generally, the second interview is much less formal, with both parties asking questions and exchanging information. I love second interviews, because that is when I really get to know the interviewee, and I think the interviewee really gets comfortable with me and the office. Then, the agent is less apt to have buyer's remorse, or the free-floating anxiety that you feel when you fear having made a bad decision.

What If the Manager Does not Want to Interview You Again?

If the manager does not feel that you match the job description of a successful agent in that office, the manager will decline to interview you again. He or she may send you a letter, and email, or text, after the first or second interview, thanking you for the opportunity to meet, and telling you that he feels you would better match the profile of another office.

This determination is in your best interests. It would be a disservice to you to go to an office that is not the best for you. The manager who cares about the tone of his/her office and about the candidate has the foresight to make those tough choices.

What If You Are Asked to Join the Office?

At any time during the first or second interview, you may be asked to join the office. If you are not sure about the office, simply tell the manager that you are not ready to make a decision. If you know, at that time, that you do *not* want to join that office, tell the manager that you do not think this office is a good match for you. The manager will appreciate your candor. No manager wants to hire someone who is not sold on the office and the manager.

Match Production Goals

Some interviewees think, even though they are not committed to fast real estate success, they should affiliate with the most productive company and office. They assume the tone and productivity of the office will give them some easy money. Unfortunately, that thinking leads to a mismatch in goals and expectations.

Managers who hire careerists have high standards for productivity. They have highly refined systems to help agents get started fast. These managers are not prepared to manage the less-committed agent. This mismatch will lead to frustration for both parties. It's important to be honest and clear about your career goals, and affiliate with an office and manager who reflects similar goals. That ensures a great start for both agent and manager.

You're Hired!

At the end of the second interview, the manager looks at you and says, "Jody, we'd really like to have you join our office. You'd be a wonderful addition to our team." You graciously accept the offer. Now, what happens? The manager will explain the steps that you will take together to:

- Activate your real estate license,
- Onboard you to the office, and
- Register you in training school.

Then, the manager will explain the start-up program for you for your first week in the business. Generally, you will be doing these activities:

- Generating leads to develop your business

- Organizing your real estate materials
- Previewing property
- Sending out new agent announcements and following up with phone calls, emails and/or texts
- Learning computer programs and other mechanical equipment and technology in the office
- Acclimating yourself to all resource information, files, and forms in the office

This is where those orientation/onboarding checklists mentioned in your interview questions come in handy. Do not expect your manager to work closely with you these first few days. You will probably be given a simple list of things to accomplish, and you will be expected to complete the assignments alone.

Summary

The interview process should be just that—a process. If the interviewer tosses a couple of softball questions to you, and then sells, sells, sells—I suggest you hold off on your decision to join. If it's that easy to be hired, what does that say about the company's commitment to your success?

You'll be using a complete process to interview and choose the buyers and sells with whom you want to work. Judge your interviewer's process against the professional standards you want to develop for your clients.

Big Ideas from Chapter 9

- Prepare yourself for the interview to make a favorable first impression—a key to being chosen by a discriminating office.
- Do a two-interview process, even if the manager hires you on interview #1. Stepping away gives you some reflection time, and you may surprise yourself with the impressions you now have.

You will think of more questions you want to ask, and now is the time to get those questions answered.

- **Principle:** The less the expectations, the lower the production.
- **Principle:** The lower the accountability, the lower the production.
- **Principle:** The more part-timers, the lower the production.
- **Principle:** Low producers drag you down. High goals and expectations inspire you to better performance (the musician's truism, too).
- Take advantage of all the ways to get information. Get visual proof of the claims you hear from your interviewer.
- Do not make your decisions based on:
    Which is the cheapest place to work.
    The fact you got hired in 15 minutes.
- Low expectations and no accountability.
- The manager is a nice guy/woman.
- You want to start at your own speed (that speed is usually translated as no money for a year...)

Most importantly, match value systems and vision. Seeing is believing. Ask for proof of the manager's claims. Your decisions are too important not to be thorough in your choice.

 ## Get a Jump-Start on Success

- Customize the five most important questions you want to ask each interviewer.
- From the five important questions and categories explored in this chapter, decide which categories and questions are important to you. Organize them to ask those questions in the interview.

- Decide the three to five most important qualities you want in a manager. Design questions to discover if that manager reflects those qualities.

- Get someone with whom to practice the interview process. Have him/ her ask you the tough questions managers should ask. Get feedback from your partner.

CHAPTER 10

You're Hired, Now What?

"Concentrate on three things: Live, eat, and breathe real estate everywhere you go and in everything you do; tell everyone you meet what you do. Brand yourself; pick a theme or a phrase with colors for advertising, etc. Make friends with and learn all you can from lenders; they are the key to closing transactions."

~Tom Raynor

In This Chapter

- What to Expect in Your First 2 Weeks in the Business
- Opportunities You May be Offered
- Attitude: It is Everything
- Getting the Best from your Manager
- Advice from Successful First-Year Agents: Five Keys to First-Year Success
- Big Ideas
- Get a Jump-Start to Success

Most experienced agents say they would have killed for the information in this chapter, because it would have saved them precious time and lots of money. Here are the principles of starting—or rejuvenating—your career to meet your goals and beyond.

What to Expect Your First 2 Weeks in the Business

Unfortunately, many agents start without onboarding, schedule, or business start-up plans. They wait for someone to

- Invite them to have a cup of coffee or lunch
- Invite them to preview homes for sale

I got both those invitations. It would be natural to conclude those activities will lead you to a sale. Wrong. Unfortunately, neither of these activities makes you any money. (Remember those business-producing vs. business-supporting activity lists?) Observing the agents in the office, I saw they were *inventory experts*. They were great at business-supporting activities. I never saw them with buyers or sellers. I quickly figured out I couldn't do things like the agents in the office did them, or I would produce the same number of sales they produced—three or four a year. (There were two other agents in the office, but I never saw them, because they were out working with real buyers and sellers, producing sales).

What Your First Week Should Look Like

Onboarding/Orientation: You followed my advice in the interview and saw or got a copy of the onboarding checklist. Your first job is to get everything done on that checklist ASAP, so you are ready to sell real estate.

Start-up Checklist: Your manager may provide a start-up or onboarding checklist, which has items on it such as "populate a database," "call potential clients," and "meet with a mortgage rep." These lists can include business-developing and business-supporting activities. Just be sure they are prioritized to start your business successfully—not just give you busywork.

Schedule Your Initial Training: Your company should have an initial training program that occurs at least every two months. Schedule attendance within your first month in the business.

Property Inspection: Every new agent wants to feel comfortable with inventory, so schedule inspection of listings for four to ten hours this week. Continue this schedule your first month. As you become comfortable with inventory, do not preview any more than you need to feel comfortable working with buyers and sellers.

 Top-producing agents preview with a reason: To do research on a potential listing, or to preview with a specific buyer in mind.

Non-producing agents have plenty of time to become "property experts."

What Your Second Week Should Look Like

Business Start-up Plan: If your manager has not provided you a business start-up plan, get one now. Start your lead generating today, devoting two to four hours a day, five days a week. Why? Because you want to generate lots of potential clients so you can choose the best ones.

Use a Proven, Prioritized Schedule: You have heard "plan your work and work your plan." Get a proven prioritized plan, work it, and review it with your coach to assure you have your activities prioritized to make money.

Your Coach: Meet with your coach at least three times this first and second week to assure you are starting your business to production fast.

 Your first two weeks create your work habits. Be sure you're on track to a productive career.

Your Training Priorities

Most companies have company training programs or programs they recommend. You should attend. You may be thinking, "I don't want to sit in those training classes. This piecemeal approach isn't in your best interest. You want the processes, systems, and continuity of thought you'll get in good training classes.

Here are specific training priorities you need in your first month in the business.

Lead Generation/Communication Skills: Learn and practice the skills of lead generation so you can begin to generate leads (which lead to appointments, which lead to clients, which lead to SALES!).

Buyer and Seller Presentations: Get the company presentations and practice them. This includes qualifying buyers and sellers. Practice 'till you're "killer." If your company does not provide presentations, there are independent companies that offer them. In today's virtual world, it is important to have great virtual buyer and seller presentations, too. Be sure you have a visual, well-organized presentation process for both buyers and sellers. By the way, practice using technology such as Zoom to give presentations so you're prepared for any type of situation.

- Business Planning Skills, including a Business Start-up Plan: Take a course that teaches you the basics of how the numbers work and gives you a method to set your goals and keep score.
- Principles of Agency and how to explain agency to a seller or buyer.
- How to complete a listing agreement and explain it to a seller.
- How to write a purchase and sale agreement and explain it to buyers and sellers.

Why these priorities? Because these either put you right on the sales path to a sale or provide the technical information you need to support those sales activities. If you do not master them right away, you will be tempted to shy away from possible commissions because you do not know how to complete these activities. You may fail to help buyers and sellers make buying decisions because you are not adept enough at sales processes and presentations.

What About Everything Else?

Yes, there is a lot to learn. Don't worry. You will be able to learn as you go. But, if you avoid getting into the field and meeting potential clients, you won't need to worry about learning more. Your money and motivation will run out before you secure that first sale. My advice here will assure that does not happen.

Is Shadowing for You?

There are some activities you may want to explore early in your career. One of these is shadowing. This literally means following a seasoned agent as he/she does business. Typically, you would shadow an agent doing a listing presentation, a buyer presentation, or presenting an offer. Is it a good thing to do? It depends on the abilities of the agent. If you decide you want to shadow, find out:

- What format the agent is going to use; is it a format that you will or have been trained to use (like an approved listing presentation)?
- What's the point of the shadowing?
- Will you get coaching on your own presentations as part of the shadowing process?
- What are you expected to provide in return?

Opportunities You May be Offered

In your first few weeks in the business, you may be offered opportunities to:

- Hold open houses for other agents.
- Co-list a property for a seasoned agent.

- Work part-time for a seasoned agent, as a buyer's agent, holding open houses, or as an assistant
- Work for a builder or a listing agent who represents a builder.

These may be great opportunities for you. Here is a closer look.

Hold Public Open Houses for Other Agents: Meet potential clients, gain experience, and leads. Before you leap at the opportunity, find out:

1. Is the home in optimum condition so potential lookers will be drawn to it?
2. Is the home in a well-driven area so you will get traffic?
3. Will the sellers leave the property during your open house? (They should not be there!)
4. Can you circle prospect the area prior to the open house? (Circle prospecting is going to homeowners in the area to invite them to the open house and ask for leads. This greatly expands your lead possibilities and open house traffic.)
5. Will you get enough open house signs (five or more) to guide drivers to the area? (More open house signs translates into much more open house traffic. It's much more effective at drawing people than an ad).
6. Can you increase that open house exposure with social media?

If the opportunity doesn't meet the six guidelines above, it may not be a good opportunity for you. It is just an opportunity for the listing agent to avoid holding the home open and/or to appease the seller.

Co-List a Property for a Seasoned Agent: When I say "co-list," I mean any kind of a commission agreement of perhaps 20 to 50 percent. This sounds like a good deal, doesn't it? But it depends on what you have to do to earn that commission. Get in writing what you will be expected to do. Too often, agents take advantage of new agents by "buying" an unpaid assistant for their listings. Be sure you can learn from this agent, and that you are doing your fair share of the work for the agreed upon commission. Get a checklist of the duties each of you will do in advance of agreeing to any kind of co-list arrangement.

Work Part-Time for a Seasoned Agent: This means you will be working essentially as an assistant. Unfortunately, this puts you into the "task-focused" business, not in the sales business. I don't recommend doing that if you want to jump-start your career.

Work for a Builder or a Listing Agent Who Represents a Builder: New agents are frequently asked by builder reps to hold open houses and/ or do administrative work for their builder listings. Before you leap at this opportunity, ask the same questions about holding open houses or working part-time for an agent. Get in writing the exact duties you will be expected to perform, the hours required, and the pay.

 BIG IDEAS Your focus should be on building your own career. The further you get from your own lead generation, the weaker your foundation.

Attitude is Everything

Although most interviewees tell me they have great tenacity and lots of self-confidence, my experience is that they give up very quickly when faced with various barriers. In fact, they mentally and emotionally get out of the business when they don't sell a home the first month. Why? Because they have their emotional thermostat set for selling a home fast. When that does not happen, they emotionally deflate and mentally quit the business.

That is why it's so important to start your business start-up plan the second week—to get an early success to keep your self-esteem high. When your self-esteem is high, you will do the hard things—lead generating and accepting rejection.

Selling a Home Fast Is the Greatest Attitude Adjustment!

When you get a sale quickly, you get noticed by management. Other people talk about you and compliment you on your success. This attention on your accomplishments makes you feel good. When you feel good about yourself, your confidence soars, so you go out and do more of those things. See Fig. 10.1, which shows you the motivational cycle.

Feeling good about yourself, you can withstand the disappointments and rejections that occur in great numbers to all real estate agents, but especially to new agents. Remember this truism? Behavior that's rewarded is repeated. It is really "self-protection" to talk to lots of people and make a sale fast. Getting that early success protects your ego from giving up and motivates you to keep on keeping on.

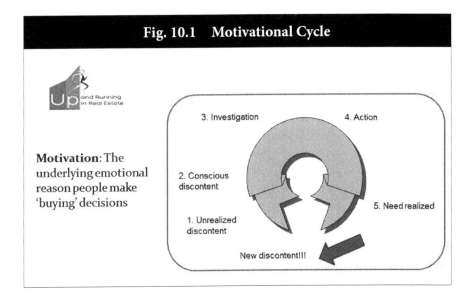

Fig. 10.1   Motivational Cycle

Motivation: The underlying emotional reason people make 'buying' decisions

3. Investigation
4. Action
2. Conscious discontent
1. Unrealized discontent
5. Need realized
New discontent!!!

Acknowledge Rejection and Move On

You are going to get lots of rejection as you start your real estate career—more than you ever have experienced before. I was a college music teacher before entering real estate sales. When I went to a party, people asked me what I did for a living. I told them I taught piano and flute performance at the college level. Boy, were they respectful of me! My self-esteem soared.

Then, I went into real estate. Same kind of people. Same type of party. Same me. Same question. My new answer: "I sell real estate". I sure got a different reaction. People treated me less warmly. They were wary, less friendly, less respectful. For one of the few times in my life, I questioned my self-worth. I was still the same person I was when I taught music. I had not become unethical, hard-sell, or untrustworthy.

It took me a few months to figure out, although the word "salesperson" has unsavory meaning to some people, it wasn't about me. You will experience the same feelings. Every new salesperson does. However, as you progress in your career, and become known as a successful real estate salesperson, people will seek you out at parties because they have learned through your actions you are an example of the best kind of salesperson: professional, caring and successful.

Ensure That Your Enthusiasm Has Staying Power

It takes only three to four weeks without results (a sale or a listing) for a new agent to feel like a failure. My survey of new agents showed a majority of agents expect to make a sale the first month in the business. That is why depression sets in so fast. What does that tell managers?

We need to help new agents into a high-numbers, activity-based business-producing plan *fast*, or they will consider themselves a failure fast. Also, you need lots of positive encouragement as you start your career. That encouragement, though, has a hollow ring to it unless it's based on what you did that day, that week and that month to create business.

Give Yourself Enough Time to Succeed

The majority of new agents surveyed gave themselves less than six months to make it. They expect to create a dynamic, successful, high-income producing business right away, or they intend to get out. However, experienced agents tell us that it takes two to three years to really reap the rewards of their hard work.

Why do those rewards come in years two and three? For one thing, experienced agents have learned the best lessons of real estate through real life. They have become much better at providing customer satisfaction. They have honed their business skills and are more technically proficient. The prospects they met in their first few months have finally become serious buyers and sellers. (Their second week in the business, they immediately created databases and a client relationship management system and populated it with these people.)

By keeping in touch with these prospects, these agents have created a gold mine of prospects for future income. How many months or years have you given yourself to create a successful career? If you go out your first day and start making sales calls, you can create a sale quickly. You will lay the groundwork for a great second year.

Be Uncomfortable to Get Comfortable

No matter what agents did before, most were comfortable and secure doing it. From the age of four, I tickled the ivories. When I started kindergarten, I played the piano for my kindergarten class as they danced and sang. All through grade school, high school, college, and graduate school, I thought of myself, and others thought of me, as a musician. I was comfortable. Even if I didn't know the answer to a musical question, I was secure saying, "I don't know."

When I went into real estate, every third sentence I uttered seemed to be, "I don't know, but I'll find out." I felt so inadequate. "Pianissimo" and "fortissimo" were just not useful as real estate vocabulary. It took three years to get as comfortable in real estate sales as I had been as a musician. You, like me, will have to tolerate not knowing. You will have to tolerate experienced agents saying things like, "You must be a newbie". There is no way around it. They will even berate you to their—or your— clients! Just smile, develop a thick skin, and move on.

My son Chris had been an agent about a year when he presented an offer on another agent's listing. When he called the other agent, that agent told him he was the top producer in his company. He asked Chris how long Chris had been in the business. Chris said, "Ten months." The agent said, "Well, you little newbie! Just do your best and don't be intimidated by me when you present your offer." How encouraging.

What that agent didn't know was that Chris had been in sales for years. He'd had great sales training in other businesses. He had a business degree from a top university. He had taken the *Up and Running in Real Estate* sales business start-up plan/training course. He had been listening to me talk about real estate for 20-some years.

Chris presented the offer. Afterward, the agent said, "Wow! Where did you get that presentation? You were really good! I would've never known you were new!" Chris told him about his background and training. We laughed about it later.

There is no reason you can't present like a great experienced agent if you have developed sales skills and have created and practiced a great visual presentation. In fact, I have trained better presenters in their first year in the business than many agents in their tenth year. It does not come naturally, though. It takes training and packaging.

The Silver Lining

Real estate is a performance art. Just like learning to drive a car, you are not as good at it the first time as you are after experiencing life on the road. That first year in real estate is really life on the road. If you dive right in, as I suggest, not only will you make money fast, but you will become technically proficient (writing purchase and sale agreements, etc.), because you will immediately put the knowledge you learned in class to work.

At the same time, you will experience great frustration, rejection, and discouragement. Think of it this way: you might as well get this learning period over with fast. These lessons, learned now, are invaluable in creating a successful career.

Getting the Best from Your Manager

You are starting your career. From this book, you can imagine the influence of your manager on your success. He/she will be:

- Helping you implement your business start-up plan.

- Providing you accountability coaching.
- Providing or managing your new agent training.

You may be fortunate and find a manager that's 100 percent committed to your success. Be 100 percent committed to that manager, too. That is a fair trade.

How can you get the best from your manager? In *Up and Running in 30 Days*, I give the ten commandments of getting the best from your manager. Here they are:

- Do the work.
- Don't argue.
- Don't make excuses.
- Don't tell the manager you've been in the business two weeks and you have a better way.
- Do thank your manager.
- Do tell other agents that you appreciate your manager's efforts.
- Do tell other new agents you meet in other companies that you have a great manager.
- Don't bug other people in the office to find another answer because you didn't like your manager's answer.
- Don't change your business start-up plan because you don't like it.
- Keep every coaching appointment.

Consider you are the junior associate and your manager is the leader. Follow the leader until you have learned the job. That is smart, no matter what business you're in.

Advice from Successful: Five Keys to First-Year Success

How can you, with your determination for career success, assure that you are getting, and staying, on the right track? I asked some successful agents—those who created strong careers in their first year—for their advice. Their comments had five commonalities. I have grouped their comments into these five critical areas:

Get a good business-start-up plan and work it consistently.

Brian Orvis: "If you don't lead generate, the potential for failing in this business greatly increases. I wish I knew how to tell other agents, in a nice way, to get the hell out of my way when they try to discourage me from proactive lead generating (cold calls by phone, expired listings, for-sale-by-owners)."

Tom Raynor: "The most important skill for a new agent is to prioritize and make the best decisions on where to allocate their time. It can be easy to wander if you wait for the business to come to you."

Connie Walsh: "Write a business plan every year, allow for flexibility, and live by it."

Advice from 50 successful first-year agents, when I asked what they wished they had more of, they said: "Business planning." With a better plan for finding buyers and sellers, they thought they could have done better faster.

Devote enough time and energy to the business from day one to create the financial rewards you need to do this job.

Marie Farnsworth: "Come to the office (go to work every day!). Go through the steps it takes to get going."

Carol Stieg: "Don't sit and wait! Get out there, meet people. Call every person you've ever known!"

Doug Nunnally: "Before your first day, create a list of all your contacts in a database."

Liz Talley: "Thank goodness I love what I do because I do it about twelve hours a day. The lunches, dinners, shopping have gone. This job can be really, really busy. To me, making substantial money is tied directly to enjoying this job. Without the financial rewards, I know my enthusiasm would drift."

Cindy Zulla: "Utilize the tools available to you. Come to work."

Connie Kruse: "Your business and your database are really similar to a living entity. You must attend to and feed them daily or they will not be healthy or grow."

Keeping the customers' best interests in mind pays dividends
Cindy Zulla: "The business is now much more customer service oriented rather than information providing. Clients need us for prioritizing the information."

Brian Orvis: "Never look at the end result (commission) before going into a listing presentation and expect to get the listing. People are more respectful of you when you are brutally honest about everything. In other words, don't give them the bunch of crap that flaky agents would use."

Connie Kruse: "Build your business on a solid foundation of systemized excellent service. Show people first how much you care, and then how much you know."

Keeping a positive attitude is up to you.
Connie Walsh: "One of the realities of real estate is facing rejection. It's important to be a part of an office team that's positive."

Chris Cross: "Get sales training. Training personally motivates me and has given me the scripts, dialogues, and systems to start my career fast."

Renee Menti: "I have some affirmations that I use daily to keep myself 'up.' One of them is, 'I have persistence, consistency, and a positive attitude.'"

Connie Kruse: "Lack of self-confidence and persistence are the two things I see new agents demonstrating that are self-defeating. Henry

Ford said, 'If you think you can or you think you can't you are usually right.' Carefully create your world and be happy."

Find a broker/manager who is as devoted to your success as you are.
From Marie Farnsworth: "Look for a manager who is enthusiastic."

From Tom Raynor: "Look for a manager who is a leader, who will be there for guidance when you need it."

From Cindy Zulla: "The best manager is one who will act as your mentor or coach. Be willing to let your manager hold you accountable to your goals."

From Connie Kruse: "An ideal atmosphere would be strong in knowledge, integrity and spirit. I researched companies to find a company that matched my values."

From Raymond Megie: "Ask for references of other new agents who started in that office. Get their opinions. Surround yourself with people who are proactive."

What Was Useful to You Here?

There it is--What I have found over the past few decades are the most important considerations for you as a future real estate success. I would love to hear what you found most useful here. What was surprising as you went through this process? What should I include in the next edition of this book? And, most of all, I would love to hear your successes!

Summary

You're hired! If you think your first days and weeks will be smooth sailing, think again! You'll be on an emotional rollercoaster. You may think about giving up real estate. That's why establishing your goals, having someone who will hold you accountable to those goals, and having a clear business track are so important.

Big Ideas from Chapter 10

Implementing your start-up plan by week two assures you make a sale *fast*—and preserves your self-esteem so you can weather the rejection and disappointment that comes with building a sales career.

Commit to creating a successful real estate career from day one. Too many agents wait to commit after they are successful—and they are never successful.

This is a lead generating business. Trying to find 'a better way' just leads to failure.

Treat your manager as you would like to be treated—with respect. You will get the best back.

Decide now how you'll manage your attitude so you keep your eye on the goal, even in the face of rejection.

Get a Jump-Start on Success

- Get through your onboarding checklist by the end of week one.
- Get a great start-up plan and implement it in week two.
- Set up an accountability coaching relationship with your manager or a professional coach.
- Start your business start-up plan your second week in the business.
- Calendar your first month in the business, placing business producing activities first so you make money fast.
- Meet with your coach often in your first month to assure you are doing the action priorities in the right order and numbers.

Resources for Success

Statistics and Trends

Profile of Buyers and Sellers, The National Association of REALTORS®, published each year.

Member Profile, The National Association of REALTORS®, published every 2 years.

Arello, The Association of License Law Officials, provides information on licensing laws internationally. Get information, too, on state licensing requirements.

Behavioral (DISC) Profiles and Interpretations

Abelson Company. Michael Abelson provides accurate, in-depth DISC results, customized for real estate agents, leadership, and staff

Real Estate Magazines

The Real Estate Professional. Independent real estate magazine.

Inman, Industry magazine

Realtor® magazine, published the National Association of REALTORS®

Education

Up and Running in Real Estate, business start-up plan with training for agents under 2 years in the business

Realtor®.com, Educational opportunities

GRI (Graduate REALTORS® Institute). Sponsored by state Realtor® associations, this National Association of REALTORS® designation is a "must" for achieving real estate professionals; three levels of courses, plus a graduate level.

CRS (Certified Residential Specialist). A Realtor® designation, this series of advanced sales courses is the next step up from GRI.

ABR (Accredited Buyer Representative). This 2-day course teaches how to represent buyers and leads to the ABR designation.

Technology Training

ePro, This is a designation from the National Association of REALTORS®. You attain the designation by taking a 2-day course in technology.

Realtor® Magazine Technology section, Training and videos

APPENDIX B

Survey Results

Expectations of New Agents—Comparison with Reality

Here are the results of a survey completed by 117 agents with fewer than 3 months in residential real estate sales. The survey results were gathered during a post-license real estate course. This survey shows the expectations of these new agents, hired as full- timers. These expectations are compared to the median income figures for REALTORS®.

1. Your expected income for this year (Figure 1 year from your practices course graduation):

   8%   expected incomes from $12,000 to $20,000

   20%   expected incomes from $21,000 to $30,000

   35%   expected incomes from $31,000 to $50,000

   30%   expected incomes from $51,000 to $75,000

   11%   expected incomes over $75,000

   When this survey was done, the median income for all REAL-TORS® (about half the licensees in the United States) was $23,100. This means that almost 92 percent of the new agents surveyed expected an income in their first year to exceed that of the median income for all REALTORS®!

Note: As I write this eBook, the median income of all REALTORS has increased to $43,300.

2. How many of sales and listings sold does this represent in your office?

Approximately one-third of those surveyed could translate their desired income into sales and listings sold.

Approximately one-third of those surveyed had no idea of what their income expectations meant in terms of numbers of homes sold.

This answer indicates that the new real estate agents surveyed are not getting the information they need to tie their income expectations to the amount of work they must complete to reach these income expectations (listings sold and sales). Without this information, agents new to the business may conclude that it is easy to make lots of money in real estate sales; just sell a few homes a year. Bottom line: They did not have a business start-up plan with these numbers projected.

3. When do you expect to receive your first check?

13%	Less than 30 days
49%	30 to 60 days
34%	61 to 90 days
4%	91 to 180 days
0%	over 180 days

It takes approximately 30 to 60 days after a sale is written for an agent to receive a paycheck. Because 62 percent of the respondents expected to receive a check within their first 60 days in the business, they intend to walk out of class and immediately sell a home! (Is it possible that they do not know the time frame involved in finding a qualified buyer?) A more realistic expectation for a paycheck is 90 to 120 days. These agents' unrealistic expectations may lead them to consider themselves failures when they do not immediately sell a home and get a quick paycheck.

4. How long can you go without income and remain in real estate?

7%   Less than 3 months

16%   3 to 4 months

30%   5 to 6 months

46%   over 6 months

Twenty-three percent of the respondents said they could go without income only 4 months or less and stay in real estate. According to a National Association of REALTORS® survey of homebuyers done at the same time as this agent survey, purchasers look for a home an average of 10 weeks before making a buying decision.

Because it takes about 1-2 months to close a home from the time the purchase agreement is written, new agents, on average, take 4 months to meet, show, and sell a prospect. Then, a home takes 1-2 months to close. That is a total of 6 months. Of course, a new agent may quickly meet a purchaser ready to buy and may be able to sell and close the home more quickly. But, the chance of finding, showing, selling, and closing a home more quickly than 3 to 4 months is remote. Are new agents' savings resources adequate to allow them the time necessary to create a strong real estate career?

5. As a first-year agent, what is the minimum number of sales and listings sold that you must complete to be retained by your manager in your office?
Seventy-one percent of the respondents did not know their managers' minimum expectations of them. Without minimum, stated productivity standards set by management, new agents do not know what is expected of them. Clear minimum

expectations and a plan to exceed them assure that both the agent and the manager are on the same track. Then, a business plan can be created, a plan that spells out the daily activities the new agent needs to complete to reach his or her stated goal and the manager's minimum productivity standards.

30 Things to Do While You are in Pre-License School to Hit the Ground Running

To download this checklist, go to:
https://carlacross.com/30-things-to-do-while-youre-in-pre-license/

What if you were organized, prepared, and educated BEFORE your first day in the business? Make your first sale faster. Here are 30 things you can do NOW to hit the ground running once you are licensed.

Managers: Use this to help your future winners literally hit the ground running!

These suggestions are excerpted from my 'tell-it-like-it-is' eBook for would-be agents, *Launching Right in Real Estate: What They Won't Teach You in Pre-License School.*

Planning and Time Management	Check when completed
1. What will your business budget be? How will you finance your first few months in real estate? (You probably won't get a paycheck your first month! (There's a sample budget in my eBook.)	☐
2. Do you have the attributes to make a success in real estate sales? Write down 6 attributes you feel are important for real estate sales success. (My attributes are listed in my eBook.	☐
3. Write down the weekly schedule you believe you should keep in real estate to be successful fast—what you're going to do and when you'll do it. See my schedule in the eBook; compare it to yours.	☐
4. Make a job description for yourself. Compare it to the one in my eBook. Ask 5 real estate agents for their job descriptions and compare them to my job description. What do the disparities tell you?	☐
5. Write your monetary and revenue unit goals for your first year in the business (sales and listings sold. How much is a 'revenue unit' worth?). Write how you will reach those goals. Compare that with the description of a 'day in the life' of a successful real estate agent as described in the eBook.	☐
6. What will your start-up costs be? Are you sufficiently 'covered' funded? To start in a professional manner? (see my eBook for my list of start-up costs. Get a list, too, from those you interview).	☐

Financial Management	
7. Get QuickBooks or other software for your financial record-keeping.	☐
8. Get an accountant. Meet with your accountant to set up your financial software and discuss how you're going to keep detailed records and receipts.	☐
9. Make a personal budget so you'll know the expenses you'll have each month, using the guide in my eBook.	☐
Lead Generation and Making Money Fast	
10. Make a list of at least 200+ people you can use as your 'circle of influence' to launch your real estate career.	☐
11. Put those people in a database (Outlook and Top Producer are examples). Consider investing in a contact management program now. Ask your interviewer about recommendations.	☐
12. Make a letter (to send snail mail, email, and or text after you're licensed) to introduce yourself and tell your 'circle of influence' you're in real estate. (a prototype letter is in *Up and Running in Real Estate*, my online training/coaching/business start-up planning program).	☐
13. Decide on 5 methods/sources of finding clients. Decide how many 'leads' you will get from these sources (In *Up and Running in Real Estate*, the online training/coaching business start-up program, we recommend 50-100 per week to assure you get paid fast).	☐

Working with Clients	
14. Gather at least 20 articles/blogs/news releases/statistics on why it's a great time to buy and sell a home. Find articles on market conditions; find research companies that provide data. Gather these resources to show buyers and sellers and educate them about market conditions. You need third party verification and substantiation!	☐
Sales and Marketing	
15. Check out real estate agent marketing sites. Put together a sample marketing plan using various resources so you can hit the ground running. *Up and Running in Real Estate* has a sample marketing plan.	☐
16. Take a sales communication course so you'll have the sales communication skills necessary to find and work with clients in real estate (such as Dale Carnegie). Please sure it has practice sessions included.	☐
17. Check out how real estate agents are using social media by visiting various sites such as Facebook, Twitter, LinkedIn, and Instagram. See agents' blogs in your area. Effective? Not effective?	☐
18. Make a social media plan using what you learned from your research of how other agents use social media.	☐
19. Which segments of the population will you work with? (first-time buyers, move-up buyers, retirees, etc.) Why? Choose your population segments and decide how to contact them.	☐
20. Which geographical areas appeal to you? Why? Choose your desired areas.	☐

Technology	
21. Make a list of the technology you believe you need, with a budget and time frame to purchase/lease it. Interview 3-5 newer agents to get their input. (Both my programs here have suggestions for the technology new agents need).	☐

Researching Real Estate Companies	
22. Go to at least 3 career nights, 'open houses' sponsored by various real estate companies. Use the interview guide in my eBook.	☐
23. Go to various agent evaluation websites (Realtor®.com, Zillow, LinkedIn, etc.). What do you see? What do you want your testimonials to say about you?	☐
24. Gather your research about real estate companies and real estate agents by checking out the Web, affiliates, (mortgage companies, title and escrow, real estate attorneys), agents, and consumers.	☐
25. Attend brokers' open houses and public open houses. Observe the agent's actions and the properties marketed by that firm. Make a list of dos and don'ts so you'll be ready for your first open house.	☐

Interviewing	
26. Using the list in my eBook, customize the 5 most important questions you want to ask each interviewer	☐
27. Decide which categories and questions are important to you from the list of 76 questions in the eBook. Organize them to ask those questions in the interview.	☐

28. Decide the 3-5 most important qualities you want in a manager. Design questions to reflect those qualities. There are qualities top agents want in a manager in my eBook.	☐
29. If you're considering peer coaching or joining a team, interview the key players first. Find out how you are paid, the training and coaching you'll receive, and accountability with your 'team leader'.	☐
Getting Educated about the Business	
30. Contact at least 3 affiliates (a mortgage person, a title person—if you have title insurance in your area), and an escrow person and find out the basics of their businesses as it pertains to working with them. Find out the services they will provide you (including marketing pieces they may have available for you to use).	☐

Launching Right in Real Estate, **from Carla Cross, literally covers everything else** *besides* **what you need to know to pass the real estate licensing exam.** *Up and Running in Real Estate* **is the 8-week 'hit the ground running' training/coaching business start-up plan for career-focused agents—includes a proven start-up plan.**

APPENDIX D

Checklists and Worksheets

Use the forms and worksheets here to plan your new career. Go to https://carlacross.com/launching-right-checklists-and-worksheets/ to grab them.

Fig. 1.1   Your Ideal Job

Check which you prefer for your ideal job.

Hours

☐ Regular Hours (no weekends or nights; you like time restrictions.)   _____

☐ Irregular Hours (like to finish a project; will work weekends, nights, if needed.)   _____

Number of hours willing to work per week: _____

Time Frame

☐ Regular Days Off and Vacation   _____

☐ You name your schedule (could work 14 days in a row, if needed, to accomplish a goal?)   _____

Amount of Independence

☐ Supervised work with task completion expectations   _____

☐ Unsupervised work; little evaluation or feedback from management   _____

Salary

☐ Steady increase based on cost of living   _____

☐ No salary (Your work determines your income)   _____

Income Potential

☐ Limited   _____

☐ Unlimited   _____

Risk/Security

☐ Low Risk (job security)   _____

☐ High Risk (no guaranteed income, but low risk of getting "fired")   _____

Comfort

☐ Little interference with private life   _____

☐ Private life can be put on hold to achieve a goal   _____

Working tasks or People

☐ Like working on tasks   _____

☐ Like working with people   _____

Work Environment

☐ Working with a group or in group activities   _____

☐ Willing to work alone (like to be self-directed)   _____

Planning

☐ Like a plan worked out for you   _____

☐ Make your own plan to achieve goals or investment you may need to get into the profession   _____

Compare your answers to the description of real estate sales and a typical job schedule.

Fig. 1.2   Self-Analysis: Attributes for Success

Rate yourself a 3 if you feel this particular attribute is a real strength of yours; 2 if you feel you're adequate; and 1 if you feel it's not one of your best qualities.

1. I do things on my own; nobody has to tell me to get going.   1 2 3

2. I finish what I start, even if it takes me more time and effort than I thought it would.   1 2 3

3. I'll tackle the challenging activities fast—I like to put myself in the action   1 2 3

4. I'm the one who plans the get-together; people look to me to organize activities.   1 2 3

5. I have accomplished things that others said I couldn't do; I knew I could.   1 2 3

6. People depend on me because I follow through on a promise.   1 2 3

7. I learn from others I respect; I put that information to use quickly.   1 2 3

8. I get excited about accomplishing something; and this causes me to keep going.   1 2 3

9. I can handle rejection without becoming devastated, because I know it's not personal.   1 2 3

10. I've created ways to do things, and have done them, even when I didn't have lots of information.   1 2 3

Weekly Schedule

Use one per week. At the end of the week, analyze your results.

NAME:

Suggested Hours Weekly:		*What You Did:*	
Lead Generating	10		hours
Qualifying buyers/sellers	5		hours
Show properties/listing properties	5		hours
Purchase/sales agreement	5		hours

How could you improve your schedule?

Evaluate Your Weekly Schedule
Rate yourself in the effectiveness of your weekly schedule:

1-10 (10 is high)

Fig. 5.6   Determine Your Normal Monthly Living Expenses

House Payment or Rent	$_____
Condominium Fees	$_____
Food	$_____
Credit Cards	$_____
Entertainment, Gifts	$_____
Savings	$_____
Dental, Medical	$_____
Car (payment, gasoline, insurance, repair)	$_____
Property Taxes and Insurance	$_____
Utilities	$_____
Incidentals	$_____
Clothing	$_____
School Costs	$_____
Health, Life Insurance	$_____
Donations, Church	$_____
Miscellaneous	$_____
Total Monthly Costs	$_____

Fig. 5.7   Total Money Required First 6 Months

Your Estimated Start-Up Expenses:	$_____
Your Estimated Real Estate Expenses Monthly x 6:	$_____
Your Other Monthly Living Expenses x 6:	$_____
TOTAL MONEY REQUIRED*:	$_____

Total money required (either savings or income) for your first six months in real estate.

Fig. 7.1   Evaluation Checklist

Affiliations

☐ None   ☐ National

☐ Regional   ☐ Other networks

Evaluation:

Specialties

☐ Products   ☐ Markets serviced

☐ Services

Evaluation:

Company image

☐ Newspaper advertising   ☐ Office Internet

☐ Signs   ☐ Social media

☐ Radio, television   ☐ Other

Evaluation:

Agents

☐ Professional demeanor

☐ Sales skills

☐ Team cooperation

Evaluate: How your background, style, people you know fit the profile of this company:

Other affiliated businesses

☐ Title companies   ☐ Banks

☐ Escrow companies   ☐ Builders

☐ Mortgage companies   ☐ Customers/clients

☐ Attorneys

Evaluation:

Fig. 9.3   Your Preferences

Selling vs. Non-Selling Manager
- ❏ You prefer a manager who doesn't sell real estate. (non-competing)
- ❏ You prefer a manager who sells real estate. (may provide a good role model/may be too busy to help you)

Training
- ❏ You prefer a formalized training program.
- ❏ You prefer to "go it on your own", with the manager available to answer questions.

Large vs. Small Office
- ❏ You prefer a large, busy office.
- ❏ You prefer a small, more laid-back atmosphere.

Large vs. Small Company
- ❏ You like the idea of a large company behind your efforts.
- ❏ You like the idea of a boutique, specialist company.

Many vs. Few New Agents
- ❏ You want to be around other new agents like you, so you prefer an office with lots of new agents.
- ❏ You want to be with seasoned agents and would rather be among the few new agents in the office.

Top Producer Assignment
- ❏ You want to be assigned to a top producer to find out how that top producer works and perhaps do work for that top producer.
- ❏ You want to become an above-average producer fast and don't want to be in the shadows of anyone else.

Age of Agents
- ❏ You want to be around people your age.
- ❏ You want to be around people of a wide range of ages and interests.

Work form Office vs. Work from Home
- ❏ You want to work from the office and have a desk at the office.
- ❏ You want to work from home.

No Supervision/Management
- ❏ You prefer little or no supervision. You'll go at your own speed.
- ❏ You want and expect leadership and guidance as you start your career.

Coach vs. No Coach
- ❏ You want a coach dedicated to your success.
- ❏ You prefer to go it alone and operate independently.

Mentor vs. Manager
- ❏ You want a mentor - someone you can go to ask questions any time.
- ❏ You want to go to your manager as your trusted adviser.

Team vs. No Team
- ❏ You are considering working with a team.
- ❏ You want to work on your own.
- ❏ You like a team atmosphere. You want to be able to go to anyone and get support.
- ❏ You prefer a "go it alone" atmosphere.

Fig. 9.7   Interview topics and questions

The Office

❏ What is your vision for your office? Your mission? (Ask to see them)
❏ What do agents specialize in here?
❏ What geographical areas does the office serve?
❏ What is your agent turnover rate?
❏ Will I get an assigned desk? If there a fee for an assigned desk?
❏ What is your average price range?
❏ What is your client profile?
❏ Are there teams in the office organized by a "rainmaker" (lead agent)? Describe them.
❏ Is there teamwork in the office? Please describe.
❏ How many transactions, on average, do new agents complete here in their first year?

Agent Profiles

❏ How many agents are in the office now? What are your recruiting goals for this year? How many do you want to hire this year?
❏ How many are less than a year in the business?
❏ How many are part-timers?
❏ What are the average number of sales per agent? Listings per agent?

In-Office Support

❏ What is your availability? Would you show me your schedule/ calendar?
❏ Do you have an assistant manager? What is his/her job description?
❏ Describe your office staff. How will they assist me?
❏ Show me the resources in the office. (Library, computers, etc.)

Support for Productivity

❏ Show me the systems and materials you have to help me promote myself. How do you distribute referrals that come into the office?
❏ Is there a fee for them?

Fig. 9.7   Interview topics and questions (cont'd)

❒ Describe your advertising policies and fees.

❒ Do you schedule floor time? How?

❒ Do you encourage agents to hold open houses? Why or why not?

Management

❒ Please describe your background, education, training, designations, and strengths.

❒ Describe how you commununicate with agents.

❒ Do you sell? What percent of your time is spent selling?

❒ Do you hire all those who interview with you? if not, how do you make your hiring choices?

❒ Describe your management style. What is important to you?

❒ Where do you see real estate in 3 years? 10 years?

❒ How do you get new information?

❒ How do you commnicate it?

❒ What are you doing differently this year? Why?

Company Profile

❒ What is the company best at? (Marketing, training, sales, etc. - companies should have one core competency that they can name easily.)

❒ What is exceptional about this company?

❒ What are its challenges today?

❒ Show me the company vision and mission.

❒ Is it a Realtor® company?

❒ How much as the company grown in the past year? Past 5 years?

❒ Describe its growth goals for the year. Next 3 years.

Marketing Strategies

❒ How does the company advertise itself?

❒ What community service strategies does the company take part in?

❒ Explain your marketing strategies as a company and the philosophy behind them.

Services Provided and Fees

❒ Describe the errors and commissions insurance coverage.

Fig. 9.7 Interview topics and questions (cont'd)

❏ Do we have access to a company attorney?

❏ How are our calls answered during weekdays; weekends answering service?

❏ What phone number is on our signs? (the agent's or the company's?)

❏ Does the company have health, dental or retirement plans available?

❏ Please provide me with a list of all costs associated with becoming an agent, a Realtor®, an agent with you.

Commission Schedules

❏ Describe your commission schedules and the philosophy behind them.

❏ Do you make some exceptions to your commission schedule - and, if so why?

❏ What is the most important service and value I'll be getting from you?

Mutual Expectations and Standards*

❏ What are your production standards for a new agent for his/her 3 months? 6 months? First year?

❏ How do you assist new agents in reaching and exceeding these standards?

❏ If you don't have standards, why not?

❏ What are my consequences if I don't meet those standards?

❏ What are the production standards of experienced agents?

❏ Are there agents here who aren't reaching standards*? How many?

❏ What are the consequences if an experienced agent does not meet standards?

❏ Do you have a program to help experienced agents meet and exceed standards?

Standards are not goals. They are minimum expectations.

About the Author

Carla Cross, CRB, GRI, MA

As a new real estate agent, Carla Cross had no sales background, training, coaching, and little guidance. She had to figure out how to sell on her own. She did, selling 40 homes her first full year in real estate. In her third year in the business, she was honored as one of the top 1% of her 400-agent company.

Although her success record is noteworthy, Carla thought there must be an easier way to achieve than her 'baptism by fire'. When her company started a training program, she jumped at the opportunity to help new agents. Then, she created fast-start training programs for the real estate agents who joined her as she went into management. She found her new agents who completed her programs succeeded fast at a high level. Several were honored in the top 10% of the company in their first year in the business.

The training programs Carla created were developed and test marketed 'in the trenches' with real agents and a hands-on manager—Carla. No theory here. There are other unique differences in Carla's programs.

1. They are designed as a *systematic, step-by-step approach* to developing businesses. One program builds to another (*Launching Right in Real Estate* precedes and introduces *Up and Running in Real Estate*) so there is no confusion or indecision as to what needs to be done. Consistency ensures success.

2. They are designed with a nod to her background as a performing and teaching musician. They reflect how real agents start their businesses with a progressive approach. *Real estate is a performance art, not a knowledge pursuit.*

Accomplishments in Coaching, Training and Speaking

Carla has taken her experience as a successful salesperson, training program author, instructor, and manager to the worldwide stage. She is one of the best-known trainer of trainers and program authors in the business. She shares her productivity principles with real estate leadership internationally.

Real estate Teaching Achievements and Awards

- Vice president of Professional Development for Windermere Real Estate, 5th largest regional firm in the U. S.: Created largest clock hour accredited training program in the Northwest for Windermere Real Estate—wrote 30 clock hour approved courses, trained 30 instructors

- Named Washington Real Estate Educator of the Year

- Named a National Realtor® Educator of the Year

- CRB master level instructor for 12 years

- Member, International Faculty of Keller Williams International; chosen to teach Train the Trainer for KW International

- Wrote or co-wrote 4 CRB credentialed programs

- Accredited to teach the Instructor Development Workshop and Train the Trainer distance learning course in the state of

Washington; these courses approve instructors to teach clock hour approved courses

- Speaker, 16 consecutive National Realtor® Conventions, all on management subjects (training, coaching, and recruiting)

Resources and Training Programs

Several of Carla Cross's real estate training books are published internationally by Dearborn Publishing, and are used as college texts. These programs are also used as training and coaching tools by some of the largest real estate companies in the world.

More of Cross's programs are endorsed as best of their kind by the Managers' Council (CRB) and Certified Residential Specialist Council (CRS) than any other trainer today.

Her best-known book for new real estate agents, *Up and Running in 30 Days*, is now in its 6th edition and is used by real estate agents worldwide to launch their careers successfully.

Carla Cross Coaching

In 2003, Carla Cross put her three decades of coaching and training to work to create a unique coaching approach. There are three distinct coaching tracks:

- *Up and Running in Real Estate,* online business planning/coaching/training for agents under two years in the business
- *Leadership Mastery* coaching, one-on-one program for managers and owners
- *Trainers' Masterminds,* small group trainers' coaching

Catch the latest in training, coaching, and leadership trends and skills in Carla's blogs:

Management in a Minute https://getarealestatecoach.com/

Up and Running in 30 Days https://upandrunningin30days.com/

Join Carla's Community at https://carlacross.com for newsletters, complimentary training tips, and special offers exclusively for members.

Bring Carla to your Association or Company

Live or virtual: Carla brings her proven sales, leadership and training principles to you.

Call her at 425-392-6914.
Email her at carla@carlacross.com.

See all events, presentations, and trainings at https://carlacross.com
Carla Cross Seminars, Inc.
1070 Idylwood Drive SW
Issaquah, WA 98027

Made in the USA
Columbia, SC
08 November 2021